Integra lex aequi custos rectique magistra
Non habet affectus sed causas iure gubernat.

THE WAR BOOK OF GRAY'S INN

Harry Dixon & Son, London, Photogravure.

Gray's Inn in 1914.

THE WAR BOOK OF GRAY'S INN

Containing Names of Members who served, with Biographical Notices of those who fell; Speeches in Hall on various occasions; and an Introduction descriptive of the activities of the Society during the War.

WITH A PREFACE BY

THE RIGHT HON. THE VISCOUNT BIRKENHEAD

COMPILED BY ORDER OF THE MASTERS OF THE BENCH FOR THE INFORMATION OF MEMBERS OF THE HOUSE NOW AND HEREAFTER

PRINTED BY RICHARD CLAY & SONS, LIMITED, AND PUBLISHED BY ORDER OF THE MASTERS OF THE BENCH BY BUTTERWORTH & COMPANY. MCMXXI

CONTENTS

LIST OF ILLUSTRATIONS

PREFACE

THIS book is an attempt to compile a short record of the activities of Gray's Inn and of its members during the Great War.

The Masters of the Bench would not be willing to incur the charge that they claim any merit greater than belongs to countless associations and to millions of individuals throughout the Empire.

Their object is not to exalt the Inn, still less themselves, but to preserve an authentic memorial for those who come after them in the House of the life which was there lived during these fateful years, and of the part which was played by its members individually, and by the House in its corporate organisation.

Let me speak of the greatest first. The young students and barristers of the Inn did not wait for the stimulus of compulsion. They went at once. They served, they won distinction, and many died in every part of the world. The noble memorial which the Chapel owes to the generosity of Master Mattinson will preserve their names to remote antiquity. But it is proper that some fuller account should be given, while the facts are still easy to collect, of those lawyer soldiers whose valour will for all time be looked upon as one of the principal glories of the House.

A very interesting chapter might be written upon the actual contribution made by the legal profession as a whole to the combatant strength of the Empire. Nor would the distinction thereby disclosed be diminished if those who volunteered were separately enumerated from those who became soldiers under one or other of the Conscription Acts. For there was surprisingly little material left in the legal profession upon which these Acts could, or in fact did, operate. It would, therefore, be repugnant and unnecessary to claim any special pre-eminence for the sons of this House. They showed the same spirit, careless of consequence to person and to career, which was shown by all young lawyers of their generation in Great Britain. More than this no one could do, and more need not be claimed. *Non carebunt vate sacro.*

Different occasions of service remained to the older members of the Society individually and to the House itself as an institution. These were very various. And here again it is necessary to make it plain that no special merit of any kind is claimed. Our motive is merely to discharge the pious duty of collecting the material which will enable those who follow us in this House to know what manner of life was lived there throughout these stirring days. And it would not seem too sanguine to hope that the matter collected in this volume will be of deep interest in future generations to those who inherit the affection which all Gray's Inn men feel for their Alma Mater. And this affection is very deep. For we are bold enough to believe that many circumstances, amongst which I would specially single out our remoteness of situation and the intimacy of our small brotherhood, have produced a higher degree of loyalty to the House than it would be reasonable to look for in institutions which so greatly exceed ours in numbers and in material pageantry. This spirit, upon which we are accustomed to pride ourselves, was illustrated as long ago as the year 1454. We find Sergeant Billing in the Paston Letters observing to Master Ledam:—

" I wylde ye schull do wyll be cause ye ar a felaw in Grays In wer I was a felaw."*

We are, therefore, more fortunate than most compilers, for we are sure already of a great company of readers who will treasure that which we have compiled, and we are also sure

* I am indebted for this passage to the industry of Canon Fletcher, formerly Preacher of the Society.

that, as long as that House, the beginnings of which may probably be traced in the reign of King Edward III, shall endure, we shall find readers who will be grateful for our labour, without the inclination to become harsh critics of the method in which we have discharged it.

The matter may be made very plain by an illustration. Gray's Inn played a constant and patriotic part in the great Napoleonic struggle. What would not we in our generation give for a record, similar to that which we now put forward, of that which happened in the course of that long struggle? Such a record would not merely be of intimate interest to all the members of the Society, it would also possess high value in the history of legal institutions in this country. If we go further back, members of this House played a part which, though bitterly controversial, was influential and decisive both in the Civil War, and in the semi-legal proceedings which were followed by the execution of King Charles I. Here again a contemporary record, had such a one been attempted, would have been a priceless addition to the historical treasures of the House.

We present, therefore, in these pages a varied collection of effort and of activity. We enable those loyal members of Gray's Inn, who will assuredly not be lacking centuries hence, to re-people quadrangles, grown even more ancient, with the ghostly figures of khaki battalions conforming to the maxims of a drill book long since obsolete, but animated by a spirit which in these Isles will never die. With very little imagination such a one will be able to recreate the swift transformation of the whole Inn into a hive of military industry. He will vividly appreciate the very spot where a German incendiary bomb so nearly wrecked the beautiful hall in which Bacon often dined and Queen Elizabeth loved to witness the revels. He will be reminded of novel guests gladly entertained for a period of many months when distressed and fugitive Belgian barristers ate their commons side by side with others to whom age or infirmity had denied combatant service.

And he will read, too, of great concourses of statesmen who assembled more than once—sometimes in moments of deep gloom—round the tables of Gray's Inn, austere as became the necessities of the times, to offer words of encouragement to a harassed but unconquerable nation.

I do not in this place single out any of those other matters which will be found more fully set out in the pages which follow. Gray's Inn did neither better nor worse than other associations of loyal Englishmen. But her sons did well and worthily of the honour and name of their House.

BIRKENHEAD.

INTRODUCTION

It has been thought convenient to preface the records contained in this volume by a short account of the history of Gray's Inn in relation to the War during the years 1914–1919. The workings in time of War of a small community dedicated to the arts of peace will not only be of interest to its present and future members, but will also have a value for those who seek hereafter to review the effect of the War on organised society within the Empire. A later generation will at least have no doubt as to the spirit in which English lawyers sought to obey their country's call in a War in which the very foundations of law were imperilled.

The arrangement of this introduction is largely chronological, but occasionally opportunity has been taken to complete a story once begun, even though the events comprising it were not confined to one year. Some of the terms employed, although familiar enough to every Member of the House, may sound strangely in a layman's ears. It may therefore be advisable to explain that the Judges and Barristers who form the governing body in all the Inns of Court are known as Masters of the Bench. The meetings of the Bench for the transaction of the business of the Society are in Gray's Inn called Pensions, and the resolutions adopted there are termed Orders of Pension. The Treasurer is a Master of the Bench who while serving that office—to which he is elected annually by Order of Pension—may be said to be the President of the Society.

1914

The year 1914 found the Society prosperous and active. Master Sir Richard Atkin (now Lord Justice Atkin) held the office of Treasurer. Great Grand Night of Trinity Term, held on June 25th, with the Earl of Halsbury as the principal guest, had been followed on the 2nd of July by a ball at which five hundred guests were present. No shadow of the impending calamity darkened these festivities.

The commencement of the Long Vacation on August 1st was followed three days later by the Declaration of War with Germany.

At a Special Pension on the 10th of September the Bench met to consider what contributions should be made by the Society to "patriotic and charitable funds in connection with the War." This was the Society's first projected War measure. And it was resolved to refer to the Finance Committee the whole question of the most effective methods to be adopted by the Society for "rendering assistance in the present national emergency."

At a Pension held on the 7th of October this Committee presented a comprehensive report, which was adopted. The report made it clear that the Society must, as a consequence of the War, face a considerable diminution of revenue, and that any contributions made to National Funds or on behalf of War objects, must be found by the introduction of drastic economies. Definite recommendations were made in this connection. Grand Nights were not to be celebrated. The dinners throughout the Hall were to be frugal. The consumption of wine was to be reduced. Measures were also considered to assist members of the Society who might be impoverished by the decline of their practice in consequence of the War. In the event few claims were made upon the Society in this respect.

One project of the Committee came to naught. It was the view of the Board of Trade that after Christmas 1914 there would be great unemployment in the building trade, and in order to help to alleviate the suffering anticipated, the Bench decided to begin in the New Year certain considerable building works in the Inn which were in contemplation before the War. It soon became clear, however, that the real problem would be a shortage rather than a surplus of Labour. The Board of Trade withdrew the circular on which the Bench had proposed to take action, and the building operations in question were therefore never launched. Otherwise the Society at once proceeded to adapt and lend its organisation to the demands of the War and to offer all possible help and countenance to War measures.

On the 19th of September Mr. Lloyd George, then Chancellor of the Exchequer, addressed a great meeting of Welshmen at the Queen's Hall, Langham Place, with a view to raising a force of London Welsh. The call made by the Chancellor of the Exchequer was answered with enthusiasm, and it was resolved to recruit at once a London Welsh Battalion.

The work of organisation was placed in the hands of a Committee of Welshmen resident in London, of which Captain Ivor Bowen, K.C., a Master of the Bench of Gray's Inn, was a leading member. During the autumn of 1914 the 1st London Welsh (known as the 15th Battn. Royal Welch Fusiliers) was raised and trained in the Inn. Over 1400 recruits were enlisted and drilled in the gardens and squares. All officers of the Battalion were made honorary members of the Bar messes at luncheon in Hall. An orderly-room, armoury and stores were provided by the Bench and throughout the War the work of organising and equipping the London Welsh Battalions was largely carried on within the Inn. Captain Ivor Bowen, K.C., promoted Major in October, 1914, and afterwards Lieut.-Colonel, was in command of the Headquarters Depot of the Battalion in Gray's Inn.

But though their Recruiting Headquarters remained in Gray's Inn, the 1st London Welsh left for France at the end of 1915, and won much distinction in the battles of the Somme and in Flanders. In particular, at the Battle of Pilckem in July, 1917, they achieved great renown in their fight with the *élite* of the Prussian Guards, the Kaiser's " Cockchafers."

In October, 1914, it had come to the knowledge of the Bench that many members of the Belgian Bar, refugees from their country, were living in London with no common meeting-place, and many of them in straitened circumstances. The Bench therefore resolved to invite all Belgian Avocats temporarily resident in London to be the guests of the Society at the daily luncheon served in Hall for Members. And for more than two years, beginning on the 2nd November, 1914, Gray's Inn Hall was at the luncheon hour a rendezvous for Belgian Avocats in London, until rationing difficulties and the general suspension of the communal life of the Society unfortunately made it impossible to continue this hospitality.

In *The Book of Belgium's Gratitude*, published in 1916, Maître Charles Bauss, Ex-President of the Federation of Belgian Avocats, makes graceful allusion to these gatherings: "We shall always remember (he says) the happy hours passed in the company of our English confrères, and more especially those we enjoyed in the historic Hall of Gray's Inn, with its marvellous wood panelling, where Queen Elizabeth danced, and which, almost 400 years later, has now become the refuge and meeting-place of those Belgian barristers who had escaped from the tyranny of foreign domination. It was in this Hall that we have found ourselves shoulder to shoulder with our English friends and brothers, and have met one another from time to time, finding comfort and consolation in discussing the affairs of our beloved country across the sea."

It should here be added that during the Long Vacation of 1919 the Bench of Gray's Inn were invited by the Bâtonnier of the Brussels Bar (Maître Theodor) and the Bar of Belgium to send a deputation to be present at the re-opening of the Cour d'Appel in Brussels. The invitation included a round of entertainments at Brussels, Antwerp and elsewhere, which the charming hospitality of the Belgian Bar suggested. The Bench gladly accepted the invitation and all arrangements were made for the visit. Unfortunately the railway strike of October, 1919, began on the day appointed for the journey, and the visit had to be abandoned—very much to the regret of the Masters of the

Bench, who had looked forward with much pleasure to meeting their Belgian confrères.

The great appeal of Lord Kitchener for men was made in the early autumn of 1914. The response of the members of Gray's Inn was prompt. By the 1st of December it was known that more than fifty per cent. of those students of the Society keeping terms who were eligible for military service were actually serving with the Forces of the Crown. But this, as it proved, was a great under-estimate of what the youth of Gray's Inn was doing. In the course of time information became more complete, and it is now possible to say that out of nearly two hundred students who kept the Trinity Term of 1914 ninety-eight were eligible for military service according to the standards of that year, and of that number as many as seventy-four were actually serving by the end of the year.

It is not possible to compute so closely the number of Barristers of the Society who volunteered for Service during this year. Their opportunity according to the standards of 1914 was more restricted, and many of them were practising overseas, but as the War went on and older men became eligible, Barristers of the Society volunteered in great numbers, until at the end of the War the Bar of Gray's Inn claimed two hundred and fourteen of the three hundred and sixty-five names which finally appeared on the Roll of Honour and the Roll of Service of Gray's Inn.

1915

On the 1st of January, 1915, Master Sir William Byrne, K.C.V.O., C.B., entered on the first (as it proved) of two years of office as Treasurer.

Towards the end of 1914, the Bench had resolved to take the initiative in forming a Battalion of Volunteers in the Borough of Holborn from men above the then military age or not at the moment eligible for service. The Mayor of Holborn (now Sir James Parker) convened a meeting, which was held at the Connaught Rooms, Great Queen Street, on the 21st of January, 1915, in support of this movement. The speakers, in addition to the Mayor, included Sir Arthur Conan Doyle and Mr. M. W. Mattinson, K.C., a Master of the Bench. The Society made a substantial contribution to the fund which was established at the meeting to provide equipment. The open spaces of the Inn were offered and accepted as the drill ground of the Battalion, office accommodation was also provided, and Benchers, members and servants of the Society, as well as many of the leading tenants in the Inn, joined the force then raised, and for many months afterwards devoted themselves to a movement which at the outset had many and great difficulties to face. The Battalion was originally known as "The Holborn Volunteer Training Corps," and the first drill took place in Gray's Inn Square on the 2nd of February, 1915.

The following members of Gray's Inn were Officers of the Battalion :—

Sir William Patrick Byrne, K.C.V.O., C.B. . (Honorary Commandant).
(A Master of the Bench)

Mr. Montagu Sharpe, K.C. . . . . . (Honorary Commandant).
(A Master of the Bench)

Lieut.-Col. Sydney Ashley, V.D. . . . . (Commanding Officer).

Sir Lewis Coward, K.C. . . . . . (Company Commander).
(A Master of the Bench)

Mr. A. E. Dunphie . . . . (Company Commander).

Mr. M. W. Mattinson, K.C. . . . . . (Platoon Commander).
(A Master of the Bench)

Mr. R. E. Dummett . . . . . (Platoon Commander).
(Now a Master of the Bench)
Mr. J. L. Crouch . . . . (Instructor of Musketry).

It is recorded of this Battalion that before the Derby Scheme or Compulsory Service was thought of, several hundred members were enlisted and passed from and through its ranks into the Regular Army. Thirty-three commissions in the Army were obtained by members of the Corps, viz.: Captains 5; Lieutenants 10; Second-Lieutenants 18. Two of the Lieutenants were gazetted direct to the Irish Guards, and one, who had shown great promise as a Bombing Instructor, was sent to the Front in charge of the Bombing Party of the Irish Guards. This officer, Lieutenant Synge, was twice mentioned in dispatches, received the Military Cross and was killed in action. Of the thirty-three officers, thirteen were drawn from the sergeants' mess of the Battalion. One received the Military Cross and the O.B.E. Two other officers received the Military Cross, and one the Military Cross and Bar. One other officer was killed in action.

The Corps, relatively to its opportunities, attained a high degree of efficiency under the command of Colonel Ashley, and in the middle of 1916 the War Office officially recognised it as a military unit and Army equipment and clothing were thereafter issued from Government stores. Afterwards military duties were assigned to it, and the General Officer Commanding the Lines of Communication allotted to the Battalion (which finally became known as the 6th County of London Volunteer Regiment) a definite part in the scheme for the defence of London. The Corps was disbanded shortly after the Armistice.

The illustration which appears on page 60 shows a muster of the Battalion in Gray's Inn Square. On the left of this picture appears a small contingent of nurses. These were members of the National Ambulance Corps which had its Headquarters in Fulwood Place, Gray's Inn. The Corps was attached to and formed part of the Volunteer Battalion, and a detachment was on duty whenever the Battalion paraded.

A tablet in the wall of No. 1, Gray's Inn Square records very briefly the work of the Battalion by the following inscription :—

THE GREAT WAR. 1914–1918

IN THIS SQUARE WERE
TRAINED THE MEN RAISED
BY GRAY'S INN AND HOLBORN
FOR SERVICE IN THE 6TH BATTN.
VOLUNTEER REGIMENT
UNDER COMMAND OF
LIEUT.-COL. SYDNEY ASHLEY, V.D.

It may be of interest to mention that a reference to the Minutes of Pension shows that on the renewed outbreak of war with France in 1803 the gardens and part of the premises of the Society were then freely handed over for military purposes, as now happened one hundred and eleven years later. In 1803 Sir Samuel Romilly, at that time Mr. Samuel Romilly, K.C., was Treasurer of Gray's Inn, and in the August of that year, upon the application of the St. Andrew and St. George Volunteer Corps, the use of the Hall under certain restrictions was allowed as an armoury and the gardens as a drill-ground. A few months later, in the same year, Lord Reay, as Lieut.-Colonel Commanding the Corps of Loyal North Briton Volunteers, applied to the Bench for the use of the gardens for " the muster and exercise " of that Corps. This was conceded conditionally upon arrangements with Colonel Reader, the Commandant of the St. Andrew and St. George Corps, to prevent the drilling of the two bodies clashing. In 1915 and the following years there were similar arrangements between the Commanding Officers of the Welsh Battalions and the Holborn Volunteer Battalion, who, as already explained, had a joint use of the Gardens and Squares for all purposes of " muster and exercise." And so history repeated itself.

Throughout 1915 various Committees were busy developing the War measures instituted in 1914. In particular the work connected with the London Welsh Battalions grew apace. In February the 1st London Welsh had been fully completed in numbers and drafted for Divisional training to North Wales.

The Army Council then authorised the formation of the 2nd London Welsh (18th Battn. Royal Welch Fusiliers). This was also raised in Gray's Inn, and altogether 3500 men were recruited in the Inn up to September, 1916. In the summer the Headquarters of the Battalion, then 1200 strong, moved to Kinmel Park, North Wales, but recruiting was steadily continued at the Gray's Inn Depot. Ultimately it was turned into a Reserve Battalion, which supplied drafts amounting to many thousands to every battle front. Throughout, this Battalion remained under the command of Master Lieut.-Colonel Ivor Bowen, K.C.

It is perhaps worth while to record what parts of the Society's premises were by the summer of 1915 occupied for War purposes. In every case the Chambers were offered by the Bench rent free, and in most cases the necessary equipment and service were provided. No. 6, Gray's Inn Place formed the Headquarters of the London Welsh Battalions. No. 7, Gray's Inn Place was lent to the Northern District Committee of the London Munitions Board. No. 10, Gray's Inn Place housed the Medical Officer of the London Welsh. At Nos. 3 and 5, Verulam Buildings sets of offices were given over—one as an orderly-room and one as an armoury—to the Holborn Volunteer Battalion. In addition, Gray's Inn Gardens became the barrack square of the London Welsh and the Holborn Volunteer Corps. Nine hundred men were sometimes mustered there at one time. As a necessary result the ancient turf of the Gardens was destroyed. Since the War, grass has been sown and it is hoped in course of time to restore to the Gardens their historic appearance.

The autumn of 1915 was marked by the first Zeppelin raids on London, and Gray's Inn, as events proved, came within one of the areas on which the enemy concentrated his more persistent attacks.

On September 8th, a Zeppelin (L.13, Lieut.-Commander Mathey) dropped an incendiary bomb on the terrace of the Gardens, doing, however, no damage apart from some slight injury to one of the old plane trees. At the same time an explosive bomb fell on a two-storied building in Jockey's Fields, only a few feet outside the Western boundary wall of the Inn. The explosion broke every window in the whole length of Raymond Buildings and shattered most of the window-frames.

The Inn was again attacked by a Zeppelin on the night of the 13th of October, when the Society escaped an irreparable disaster by a hair's breadth. About 9 p.m. an explosive bomb fell in the Gardens ten feet from the west wall of No. 4, Gray's Inn Square. It opened a breach in the wall of that house at the ground-floor level some ten feet wide by eight feet high. About forty window-frames were driven in from their settings. The interiors of the ground-floor and first-floor rooms in three houses abutting on the Gardens were entirely wrecked. By some lucky chance no personal injury was done to any resident of the Inn, either then or at any other time.

It has since been ascertained that this particular raid over the centre of London was carried out by Lieut.-Commander Breithaupt in L.15. He is reported to have dropped twenty-seven high explosive and eleven incendiary bombs "in the centre of London." As he passed from South to North one of his high explosive bombs nearly destroyed the Lyceum Theatre, another wrought considerable devastation in Lincoln's Inn, including the destruction of the glass of the Chapel, and a third the mischief already described in Gray's Inn Gardens.

This last great missile was accompanied by a shower of incendiary bombs which Breithaupt must have discharged as soon as he arrived over Gray's Inn. Within two or three seconds no less than six fell in or near South Square. One of the six struck the roof of No. 14, South Square and buried itself beneath the tiles without igniting. The same inglorious fate befell another which landed in the Gardens. A third broke the pavement-box of an electric-light cable against the wall of No. 12, South Square. Two more fell about the centre of South Square within ten yards of one another. An eyewitness describes these bombs as "burning themselves out in two great mounds of fire which lighted up the whole quadrangle. To one standing in the Square the change from pitch-black darkness and the noise of distant bombing to this sudden blinding light and the crash of the explosive bomb seemed for a moment to be something supernatural."

The last of the bombs almost produced a catastrophe. It fell on the roof of the Benchers' Robing-room—a small single-storied apartment built on to the Hall—piercing the roof and afterwards becoming embedded in the floor. The same eye-witness says: "A few seconds sufficed to make this room a furnace. The open door showed nothing but one white sheet of rolling flame." It is now permissible to say that the escape from destruction of the Great Hall of the Society was almost miraculous. Only a thin brick wall separated the Benchers' Robing-Room from the oak panelling which lines the interior of this ancient building. Fortunately the hour of the night was early, ready help, headed by the Housekeeper, Charles Sansom, was available, and streams of water were at once poured on to the bomb through the hole which its passage had made in the flat roof of the Robing-room, and in this way the fire was extinguished. The charred remains of the bomb have been preserved. Had it been of the explosive type the side of the Hall must have been blown in, or had this bomb fallen three yards to the north it must have pierced the magnificent Tudor roof and, igniting the 350-year-old rafters, set the whole Hall aflame.

From October, 1915, until December, 1917, the Inn escaped further injury, although on three occasions lives were lost and great damage was done by bombs which fell within a few yards of its boundaries.

On the 18th of December, 1917, however, an explosive bomb of the type known as an aerial torpedo, weighing 110 lbs., was dropped by a Gotha aeroplane and fell on the roof of No. 6, Gray's Inn Square. It did not explode, but pierced the house from roof to cellar, and striking the cellar floor, burrowed its way nine feet below. It then turned horizontally for five feet, and was found lying on its side when it was dug out by men of the Royal Engineers next day. By a fortunate chance the four sets of Chambers traversed by the bomb were not occupied that night.

From September, 1914, until the Armistice Gray's Inn was guarded by a force of special constables, composed of some officers and servants of the Inn, with two or three of the tenants.

The Force had charge of nearly fourteen acres of what proved to be one of the vulnerable parts of London. They organised their own Fire Brigade, and when the Hall, as above recorded, was threatened with destruction, they extinguished, without the help of the Metropolitan Fire Brigade, who were urgently required elsewhere, the bomb which would otherwise have caused irreparable damage.

It was during this year that the Bench ordered the removal of the valuable stained glass in the Society's Hall. It was taken down piece by piece, carefully packed, and stored in deep cellars underneath the Hall. It has now been replaced. As already mentioned, the glass in Lincoln's Inn Chapel was destroyed on October 13th, 1915.

In November, 1915, a Memorial Service was held in the Chapel of the Society for those members of the Inn who had already given their lives in the service of their country. At that time the known number of the fallen was nine. It was to be increased to forty-four before the Armistice.

In Easter Term of this year the last Moot was held during the War. In the same year the Society, recognising that all eligible candidates were serving with the Forces, suspended the granting of the Society's Bacon and Holt Scholarships for the period of the War.

1916

Sir William Byrne was re-elected Treasurer for the year 1916.

Judged merely by the Minutes of Pension the year might seem barren of events relating to the War. The Society was indeed deserted by most of its members. Its young men were occupied elsewhere; but those who remained here were able to say that never within living memory had it been a busier place, and particularly in respect of matters appertaining to the great struggle. Its precincts—squares—gardens—buildings—were thronged with troops. It was noisy with words of command. A military band played martial music. Squad drills, inspections, pay parades, were the ordinary events of the week.

A sentence from Hawthorne (*English Note Books*, ii, 581) brings into sharp relief the changes which the War had wrought: ". . . . Gray's Inn, a great quiet domain, quadrangle beyond quadrangle, close beside Holborn, and a large space of greensward enclosed within it. Nothing else in London is so like the effect of a spell as to pass under one of these archways and find yourself transported . . . into what seems an eternal Sabbath." It was no Sabbath during the War.

In May, 1916, the Right Hon. William Morris Hughes, Prime Minister of the Commonwealth of Australia, was elected an Honorary Bencher—a compliment which nine years before had been paid to Sir Wilfrid Laurier and Mr. Deakin. The election was held immediately before a House Dinner, when Mr. Hughes took his place at the High Table in a "Hall" which included many Barristers and Students on leave from the various Fronts. It is to be regretted that no record was kept of the speeches made at this dinner, but the spirited speech of Mr. Hughes evoked great enthusiasm.

Three years afterwards, in the Treasurership of Lord Birkenhead, Mr. Hughes, who was and is Attorney-General, as well as Prime Minister of the Commonwealth of Australia, presented himself for admission as a Student of Gray's Inn, and after his admission was immediately called to the Bar. On the same day he received from His Majesty his Patent as an English King's Counsel. It is doubtful if there is on record another instance of a gentleman being admitted a student, called to the Bar, and made one of His Majesty's Counsel, all on the same day.

On July 31st, 1916, the Right Hon. H. E. Duke, K.C., M.P., a Master of the Bench, accepted the office of Chief Secretary to the Lord Lieutenant of Ireland. And on October 23rd, 1916, the Treasurer (Sir William Byrne) was appointed Under-Secretary to the Lord Lieutenant. In January, 1917, Master Sir James Campbell, K.C., M.P., was appointed Lord Chief Justice of Ireland, and in June, 1918, he became Lord Chancellor of Ireland. Master A. W. Samuels, K.C., M.P., succeeded Master Sir James Campbell as Attorney-General for Ireland in April, 1918; and to complete the tale of Gray's Inn's connection with Ireland in these eventful times, it may be mentioned that another Master of the Bench, Sir Hamar Greenwood, Bart., K.C., M.P., now holds the office of Chief Secretary for Ireland.

1917

On the 1st of January, 1917, Sir William Byrne was succeeded in the office of Treasurer by the Right Hon. Sir Frederick Smith, K.C., M.P., His Majesty's Attorney-General (now Viscount Birkenhead).

During the next three months the Society took its most drastic War measures. It was considered desirable to suspend for the period of the War the evening dinners in Hall. As is well known, under the Consolidated Regulations a Student keeps terms by dining in the Hall of his Inn the prescribed number of days. He must be present at the grace before dinner, during the whole of the dinner, and until the concluding grace has been said. On the 19th of December, 1916, the Bench ordered that, beginning with Hilary Term of 1917, and until further order, the dinner hour be 1.15 p.m., that grace should then be said, and the concluding grace should be said at 1.45 p.m. This enabled the few students not eligible for service to keep term.

It was, in fact, a reversion to ancient practice. Before 1713 the dinner hour of the Society was 1 p.m. By an Order of Pension made May 15th, 1713, it was enacted that "Inasmuch as the Courts of Justice sitt now much latter than formerly it is Ordered that the hour of dineing in this Society shall the next term be of 2 of the clock precisely." On May 3rd, 1782, by Order of Pension, the dinner hour was altered to 4 p.m., and by subsequent Orders it arrived at the present hour of 7 p.m.

The saving of fuel, service, light and food—all things in 1917 of vital importance—resulting from the suspension of evening dinners was very considerable.

In March of the same year the Bench decided to close the Common Rooms. This step made it possible to release for National Service further servants of the Society over military age. The Library remained open throughout the War, although early in 1915 the Librarian (Mr. M. D. Severn) joined the Forces as a private. He served with credit, and by the Armistice had been promoted a Second-Lieutenant, 6th Battn. Northamptons, and was acting as Town Major at Reumont in France. The services in the Chapel also continued without interruption. The Reader (the Rev. J. L. Phillips) at an early stage volunteered for service, and was given a commission as Lieutenant in the Ordnance Corps, where he did good work. In his absence the whole duty in the Chapel was taken by the Preacher (the Rev. R. J. Fletcher, D.D.), although Masters of the Bench assisted by reading the Lessons.

On the 12th of March, 1917, Lieut.-General the Right Hon. J. C. Smuts, K.C., arrived in this country. On the 28th of March he was entertained at dinner in Gray's Inn Hall. The proceedings were private, and no report of the speeches made upon the occasion is now available. A list of the guests is printed elsewhere, and it shows that all that was most eminent in the Profession assembled in Gray's Inn Hall to do honour to General Smuts. The invitation card contained the words "the dinner will be in conformity with the suggestions of the Food Controller," and it may now be said generally that at all the functions in Gray's Inn Hall referred to afterwards the strictest regard was had to the frugal admonitions of the Food Controller.

The chief event in Gray's Inn of the winter of 1917 was the visit of the Prime Minister (Mr. Lloyd George). The time was a very critical and anxious moment in the War, and the occasion a dinner intended to bring together in friendly social intercourse the chiefs of the newly-formed Air Force. The dinner was held on the 14th of December, 1917, and 106 Benchers and Guests were present. It will be seen from a list which appears elsewhere that the latter were representative of all branches of the Services, as well as of the Law and the great Civil Departments of the State. Mrs. Lloyd George and other ladies were present in the Minstrel Loft during the evening. A full report of the speeches at this historical gathering is printed in this volume.

The air raids against London had reached their culminating point about this period, and the Bench were not without some apprehension as to the safety of so distinguished a company in an area which was a favourite target of enemy effort. Precautions were taken—unknown to the guests—which would have proved their value if the enemy had selected the night of the 14th of December for one of his periodical raids. In fact the evening passed without any alarm. But only four nights later, on the 18th of December, as previously recorded, a large 110-lb. bomb dropped from a Gotha aeroplane smashed through adjoining premises in the Inn from roof to cellar.

Towards the end of 1917, when the wanton outrage of the indiscriminate bombing of the civilian population of London was at its height, there was a project, warmly advocated by the Press and then adopted by the Military Authorities, of placing German officers, prisoners of War, in certain areas likely to be attacked, in the hope that their presence might serve as some deterrent. Gray's Inn was deemed one of those areas and the Common Room and Lecture Room Building in Field Court was inspected by the Military and pronounced suitable for the purpose. A portion of the Gardens was to serve as an exercise ground. Fortunately for the Society the scheme was afterwards abandoned—so far as London was concerned.

1918

The Attorney-General was re-elected Treasurer.

By this time the professional life of the Inn was at its lowest ebb. There were only twenty-nine admissions in 1917. The daily luncheon in Hall was still maintained. It was indeed continued throughout the War, but with the coming of the Rationing Scheme, Meat, Sugar, Butter, and indeed all viands which were subject to the Orders of the Food Controller, wholly ceased to appear on the luncheon tables in Hall. Foods which, although not rationed, were known to be scarce and in demand in poor households were also banished. Thereafter the menu had a strange appearance and the meals were meagre. But "Hall" was still open and some Members gathered there daily, and those who were on leave knew that they might hope to meet their friends in that way. Guests were not permitted except to Members on leave from one of the Fronts.

On Monday, the 29th of July, 1918, the Treasurer and Benchers entertained at dinner in the Hall the "Ministers responsible for the Fighting Services." The Toast of the evening, proposed by the Treasurer, was "The War Cabinet." It will be seen from the list of guests set out elsewhere that four of the six members of that distinguished Body were present.

The Armistice, on the 11th of November, 1918, was followed by a Service of Thanksgiving for Victory in the Chapel of the Society on Sunday, the 17th of November. The sermon preached on the occasion by the Preacher of the Society is printed on page 93.

In December, 1918, the Hon. J. W. Davis, who had succeeded Mr. Page as Ambassador for the United States of America, arrived in England, and was entertained at luncheon in the Hall on the 20th of December. His Excellency's speech in answer to the toast of his health, proposed by the Treasurer, was not reported at the time, Mr. Davis having promised that he would make no public utterance before his appearance at the Pilgrim's

Dinner held in the same week. It is therefore published for the first time in this volume.

At the last Pension held in Michaelmas Term the Attorney-General was re-elected to fill the office of Treasurer for the year 1919. An election for a third term was not without precedent in Gray's Inn. Among former holders of the office the outstanding case is that of Francis Bacon, who became Treasurer in 1609 and continued in that position until 1617, though after his appointment as Attorney-General in 1613 he does not appear to have again presided at Pension. The following pages show that his successor in the offices of His Majesty's Attorney-General and Treasurer of Gray's Inn during the period of the Great War was by no means an absentee from the House and its activities.

When Bacon's long term as Treasurer came to an end in 1617, the Order of Pension 26 May, 1617, which appointed his successor had a preamble providing that "the Treasuror that shalbe of this house shalbe Treasuror but for one yeare only together & no longer."

This resolution, however, was only adhered to in quiet times. In times of trouble, which came before long, Treasurers held office for seven, eight and nine years. During such periods as the Civil War, Cromwell's Wars, the years of the Plague, and the Dutch invasion, the same Treasurer presided, while the storm lasted, over a somewhat discomposed community. Very different were the reasons which led to the re-election of the Treasurer during the Great War. In some degree they were personal, but undoubtedly the expedient helped to ensure a consistent policy.

1919—1920

In the first days of 1919, before the beginning of Term, the Attorney-General was appointed Lord Chancellor and raised to the Peerage under the title of Lord Birkenhead.

In March of that year the Bench invited his Lordship to give sittings for his portrait to be painted by Mr. Glyn Philpot, A.R.A., at the cost of the Society. The portrait, which shows Lord Birkenhead in his robes as Lord Chancellor, was exhibited in the Royal Academy in the ensuing Spring, and in the Autumn was hung in Gray's Inn Hall, where it now is. The picture bears the following inscription :—

THE RIGHT HON. LORD BIRKENHEAD
SOLICITOR-GENERAL 1915
ATTORNEY-GENERAL 1915–1919
LORD HIGH CHANCELLOR 1919
TREASURER OF GRAY'S INN 1917–1919.

PAINTED FOR THE HONOURABLE SOCIETY OF GRAY'S INN.

It was also resolved to give a House Dinner of the Society in honour of the Treasurer, the Lord Chancellor. This event took place on the 9th of May, and was an occasion of enormous interest and pride to all Members of the Society. In the unavoidable absence of Master John Rose, His Honour Judge Mulligan, K.C., as Senior Bencher, presided. The Lord Chancellor of Ireland, Master Sir James Campbell, Bart., came over from Ireland so that both Lord Chancellors were present, and there was an assemblage of Benchers, Barristers and Students unique in the annals of the House. A full report of the proceedings is printed on a later page.

The erection in the precincts of the Inn of a suitable memorial to the Members of the House who had fallen in the War was at this time engaging the anxious consideration of the Bench. The question was happily solved by a letter received at a Pension held on the 25th of June in which Master Mattinson,

K.C., expressed to the Bench his desire to defray the cost of a War Memorial to the Members of the Society who had fallen, to be erected in the Chapel of the Society. The offer was accepted, as was also a further offer subsequently made by Master Mattinson to complete the scheme of decoration on the north side of the Chapel by placing a window there in memory of Archbishop Sheldon, a former Member of the Society.

The Memorials finally took the form of a sculptured tablet executed by Mr. Pomeroy, R.A., and a large three-lancet Victory Window by Mr. Christopher Whall. The window which commemorates Archbishop Sheldon stands between the pulpit and the altar, and is the work of Professor Anning Bell, A.R.A. All three monuments are fully described and illustrated in a later part of this volume, but it may be said here that their beauty has done much to soften the former austerity of the interior of the Chapel. It is pleasant to record that all the stained-glass windows in the Chapel, including the well-known "Archbishops Window" above the altar, are gifts from members of the Society—save one which was presented by The Rev. J. H. Lupton, D.D., Preacher of the Society from 1890 to 1901.

The Memorial Window and Tablet were dedicated by the Bishop of Kingston at a service held in the Chapel on the 18th of April, 1920. An account of this service precedes the biographies of Fallen Members in this book.

The Society's thanks to the giver of the War Memorials are recorded in the following Pension Order, made on the 21st of April, 1920, on the motion of the Treasurer, Master Montagu Sharpe, K.C.

"Ordered that the grateful thanks of this Society be tendered to Master Mattinson for his generous gifts which have provided a Memorial worthy of the services and sacrifice of Members of the Society who fell in the late War and have permanently enriched the Chapel of this House."

From this brief chronicle of five years of War one fact emerges to epitomise the story of the Inn during the period. It may be said that within the limits of its opportunities the whole Society "served" in the War. The conflict brought disturbance to the Inn, and, as the years sped by, with the mounting toll of the Fallen, much bereavement; but it brought no confusion—and certainly no torpor. There was no "closing down." The machinery of the Inn worked at full pressure, but, like other machinery under the spell of War, it was turning out new products.

Strangely enough, the impression that remains is one of cheerfulness. For many months while air-raid alarums and excursions prevailed the precincts were "an unhealthy area" in a much-vexed city; but the Inn never lost its pleasant aspect or became deserted. Its traditional quiet disappeared, but never its traditional serenity.

SPEECHES

DELIVERED IN GRAY'S INN HALL

UPON VARIOUS OCCASIONS DURING THE WAR

AND AT

THE HOUSE DINNER TO THE TREASURER
(LORD BIRKENHEAD)

UPON HIS ELEVATION TO THE OFFICE OF LORD HIGH CHANCELLOR

MARCH 28, 1917

DINNER TO LIEUT.-GEN. J. C. SMUTS, K.C.

DECEMBER 14, 1917

DINNER TO THE PRIME MINISTER AND CHIEFS OF THE AIR FORCE

JULY 29, 1918

DINNER TO THE MINISTERS IN CHARGE OF THE FIGHTING FORCES OF THE CROWN

DECEMBER 20, 1918

LUNCHEON TO THE AMERICAN AMBASSADOR

MAY 9, 1919

HOUSE DINNER TO THE TREASURER (THE LORD CHANCELLOR)

MARCH 28*th*, 1917.

Upon the conclusion of his victorious campaign in German East Africa, Lieut.-General the Right Hon. J. C. Smuts, K.C.—alike eminent as lawyer, statesman and soldier—landed in this country on the 12*th of March*, 1917. *He dined with the Treasurer (the Attorney-General) and Masters of the Bench in Gray's Inn Hall upon the* 28*th of March, and on the occasion made his first speech after his arrival in England. It was the prelude to his splendid services to the Empire in the War Cabinet and other great places during the following years of the War, and since continued in the high office of Prime Minister of the Union of South Africa.*

In reply to the toast of his health proposed by the Treasurer, General Smuts responded in a speech of much feeling and eloquence, and conceived in the spirit of lofty patriotism which marked all his utterances and actions during the War and since.

Unfortunately no note was taken of the speeches upon the evening of March 28*th. The only record of the evening is the names of the distinguished company which met General Smuts. These appear on the table plan of the dinner on the next page.*

TABLE PLAN

The Treasurer

(The Right Hon.
SIR FREDERICK SMITH, *K.C.*, *M.P.*
(*Attorney-General*)

Lieut.-General the
Right Hon. J. C. SMUTS, *K.C.*

Master His Honour
JUDGE MULLIGAN, *K.C.*

The Right Hon. the
EARL OF DERBY, *K.G.*
(*Secretary of State for War*)

Master LEWIS COWARD, *K.C.*

The Right Hon. the
DUKE OF MARLBOROUGH, *K.G.*

Master W. T. BARNARD, *K.C.*

The Right Hon.
SIR EDWARD CARSON, *K.C.*, *M.P.*
(*First Lord of the Admiralty*)

Master HERBERT F. MANISTY,
K.C.

Admiral
SIR JOHN JELLICOE, *O.M.*, *G.C.B.*
(*First Sea Lord*)

Master ARTHUR GILL

The Right Hon.
LORD JUSTICE PICKFORD

Master the Hon.
SIR RICHARD ATKIN

Lieut.-General
SIR NEVIL MACREADY, *K.C.B.*
(*Adjutant-General to the Forces*)

The Right Hon.
SIR JOHN SIMON, *K.C.*, *M.P.*

Master F. A. GREER, *K.C.*

General
SIR JAMES WILLCOCKS, *G.C.M.G.*

Master MONTAGU SHARPE

The Right Hon. LORD FINLAY
(*Lord High Chancellor*)

Master MATTINSON, *K.C.*

The Right Hon. the
EARL OF HALSBURY

Master C. A. RUSSELL, *K.C.*

Field-Marshal the Right Hon. the
VISCOUNT FRENCH, *O.M.*, *G.C.B.*

Master the Right Hon.
H. E. DUKE, *K.C.*, *M.P.*

The Right Hon. the
EARL OF READING
(*Lord Chief Justice*)

Master EDWARD CLAYTON, *K.C.*

The Right Hon.
WINSTON CHURCHILL, *M.P.*

Master VESEY KNOX, *K.C.*

The Right Hon.
SIR SAMUEL EVANS
(*President of the Probate Division*)

General
SIR WILLIAM ROBERTSON, *K.C.B.*
(*Chief of the Imperial General Staff*)

Captain the Hon.
FREDERICK GUEST, *M.P.*, *D.S.O.*
(*A.D.C. to General Smuts*)

SIR GORDON HEWART, *K.C.*, *M.P.*
(*Solicitor-General*)

Master T. M. HEALY, *K.C.*, *M.P.*

The Right Hon.
LORD BEAVERBROOK

Master Lieut.-Colonel
IVOR BOWEN, *K.C.*

DECEMBER 14th, 1917.

On this evening the Prime Minister (Mr. Lloyd George) and the chiefs of the newly organised Air Force were the guests of the Treasurer and the Masters of the Bench.

It was one of the worst moments of the War.

Russia, in collapse, had fallen out of the War. Roumania crushed had sued for peace. Italy was reeling under the overwhelming catastrophe of Caporetto. The British Army was held up by the mud of Flanders. The United States of America seemed to be coming but slowly into the war, while Lord Lansdowne's famous letter suggested to some the doubt whether England would endure to the end.

It was in these circumstances that the uncompromising and ringing declarations of the Prime Minister in Gray's Inn Hall once more heartened the Nation and gave renewed confidence to the Allies.

SPEECHES

AT A DINNER GIVEN IN HONOUR OF THE PRIME MINISTER AND THE CHIEFS OF THE AIR FORCE IN GRAY'S INN HALL ON FRIDAY, THE 14th OF DECEMBER, 1917.

The Treasurer (the Right Hon. Sir Frederick Smith, K.C., M.P., Attorney-General) presided.

The Guests included: The Prime Minister (the Right Hon. D. Lloyd George, M.P.); the Minister for War (the Right Hon. the Earl of Derby, K.G.); the Minister of Munitions (the Right Hon. Winston Churchill, M.P.); the Air Minister (the Right Hon. Lord Rothermere); Lieut.-General the Right Hon. J. C. Smuts, K.C.; the Home Secretary (the Right Hon. Sir George Cave, K.C., M.P.); the Right Hon. Sir Edward Carson, K.C., M.P.; the Right Hon. G. N. Barnes, M.P.; His Excellency the Italian Ambassador; His Excellency the American Ambassador; His Grace the Archbishop of Canterbury; the Lord Chancellor (the Right Hon. Lord Finlay, G.C.M.G.); His Grace the Duke of Westminster, G.C.V.O., D.S.O.; His Grace the Duke of Marlborough; the Right Hon. the Earl of Halsbury; the Lord Chief Justice (the Right Hon. the Earl of Reading, K.C.V.O.); the Right Hon. Lord Dunedin, K.C.V.O.; the Right Hon. Lord Parker of Waddington; the Right Hon. Lord Sumner; the Right Hon. Lord Justice Swinfen Eady; the Right Hon. Mr. Justice Darling; the Hon. Mr. Justice Roche; Major-General the Right Hon. Lord Cheylesmore, K.C.V.O.; the Right Hon. Lord Burnham; the Right Hon. Lord Beaverbrook; Admiral Sims (Commanding U.S. Naval Forces); Admiral the Right Hon. Lord Beresford, G.C.B., G.C.V.O.; Admiral Mark Kerr, C.B., M.V.O.; Lieut.-General Sir John Cowans, K.C.B.; Lieut.-General Sir David Henderson, K.C.B.; Lieut.-General Sir Francis Lloyd, K.C.B., C.V.O.; Lieut.-General Sir Nevil Macready (Adjutant-General of the

Forces); Major-General J. M. Salmond, C.M.G., D.S.O. (Director-General of Military Aeronautics); Major-General Garnet Hughes, D.S.O. (Canadian Army); Major-General E. B. Ashmore, C.B., M.V.O.; Major-General C. A. Longcroft; Colonel Bolling (Asst. Chief of the U.S. Air Service); Brigadier-General K. T. Dowding; Brigadier-General E. L. Ellington, C.M.G.; Brigadier-General Hearson, D.S.O.; Brigadier-General G. Ludlow Hewitt, M.C.; Brigadier-General R. E. Hogg, C.I.E.; Brigadier-General F. C. Jenkins; Brigadier-General G. Livingstone, C.M.G.; Brigadier-General D. le G. Pitcher; Brigadier-General Geoffrey Salmond, D.S.O.; Commodore Godfrey Paine, C.B., M.V.O.; Captain A. S. Vyvyan, R.N., D.S.O.; Captain C. Lambe, R.N., D.S.O.; Colonel E. M. Maitland, D.S.O.; Lieut.-Colonel A. J. L. Scott, D.S.O., M.C.; Colonel S. Ashley; Lieut.-Colonel C. L. Whitburn; Commander O. Locker-Lampson, M.P.; Squadron-Commander C. H. Butler, D.S.O., D.S.C.; Commander Spenser Grey; Commander Sir Trevor Dawson, R.N.; Lieut.-Commander H. W. S. Chilcott; Major J. L. Baird, D.S.O., M.P.; Captain Wrench, D.S.O.; the Right Hon. the Lord Mayor; Lord Hugh Cecil, M.P.; Lord Edmund Talbot, D.S.O., M.P.; the Right Hon. Sir Ailwyn Fellowes, K.C.V.O., K.B.E.; Captain the Hon. Frederick Guest, D.S.O., M.P.; Sir Edward Goulding, Bart., M.P.; the Right Hon. Sir Arthur Channell; the Solicitor-General (Sir Gordon Hewart, K.C., M.P.); the President of the Law Society (Mr. S. Garrett); Sir George Lewis, Bart.; the Hon. Sir Charles Russell, Bart.; Sir A. H. Bodkin; the Treasurer of the Middle Temple (Mr. R. A. McCall, K.C.); Sir Reginald Brade, K.C.B.; Sir Luke Fildes, R.A.; Sir Paul Harvey; Sir George Riddell; Sir Archibald Salvidge; Sir William Weir; Mr. Joynson Hicks, M.P.; Mr. Harold Smith, M.P.; Mr. Urban Broughton, M.P.; Mr. J. L. Garvin; Mr. Arnold Bennett; Mr. J. T. Davies; Mr. E. S. Saunders; Mr. D. Handley Page; Mr. G. Holt Thomas; Mr. H. White Smith; Mr. T. Sopwith.

The Masters of the Bench present, in addition to the Treasurer, were: Master Henry Goudy, D.C.L.; Master His Honour Judge Mulligan, K.C.; Master M. W. Mattinson, K.C.; Master Lewis Coward, K.C.; Master C. A. Russell, K.C.;

Master the Hon. Sir Montague Lush; Master T. Terrell, K.C.; Master W. T. Barnard, K.C.; Master H. F. Manisty, K.C.; Master Edward Clayton, K.C.; Master W. J. R. Pochin; Master Arthur E. Gill; Master E. F. Vesey Knox, K.C.; Master Montagu Sharpe; Master F. A. Greer, K.C.; Master T. M. Healy, K.C., M.P.; Master C. Herbert-Smith; Master Lieut.-Colonel Ivor Bowen, K.C.; Master W. Clarke Hall; Master R. E. Dummett; Master Lieut.-Colonel Sir Hamar Greenwood, Bart., M.P., with the Preacher (the Rev. R. J. Fletcher, D.D.) and the Under-Treasurer (Mr. D. W. Douthwaite).

The toasts of "The King," "The Queen, Queen Alexandra, the Prince of Wales and the other Members of the Royal Family" were drunk. The company then rose "To the Memory of Our Members who have fallen in the War," and raised their glasses in silence. After "Domus"

THE TREASURER proposed "The Prime Minister." He said: Prime Minister, my Lords and Gentlemen. The Benchers of this Inn have the privilege of entertaining to-night a very distinguished company under circumstances which even in the long history of this Inn must be pronounced unusual. We must offer you, I think, some apology for the meagreness of the material fare which we have placed before you. We have judged it to be less important to maintain the traditions of this ancient Inn for hospitality than to set, as far as in our power, an example of the necessities in which the nation finds itself to-day; and we are sure that those who are our guests to-night, and many of whom have been our guests in happier days, will remember that we have it in our power, as at other times, to offer hospitality on a more generous scale.

The purpose of this assembly is twofold. It is a dinner held under circumstances which must be admitted by every one to be as grave as any even in the long history of this Inn, which has witnessed the development of so many threats to this country, and the destruction of so many threats to this country. There are here to-night men of the utmost distinction who carry the greatest burden of responsibility in what, perhaps, must be pronounced as the gravest crisis in which this country and this

Empire has ever found itself. The first and primary object of this dinner is to assure the man who bears the burdens of the Empire, and who supports a higher degree of responsibility than any British statesman in the whole long and glorious history of these islands has ever borne, that he has our confidence and support, and that, great as is the burden imposed upon him, we are of opinion that his courage, his resource and his imagination will not be inadequate to it.

We live in days in which those who form the Government occupy a singularly unenviable situation, for there is hardly a day, indeed there is hardly an hour, in which they are not compelled to make some new trespass upon individual comfort, and indeed some new threat even to the actual means of subsistence. There is hardly a limit to the cruelty of the demands which from day to day and hour to hour the Executive is compelled to put forward. It would be impossible for any Government to face the country from day to day with the increasing demands which we are making upon them not only in their material resources, which measured in these scales is a small consideration, but also in terms of life and blood—nothing could sustain those who, against their will, have been compelled to undertake this responsibility, except the profound conviction that no alternative road lay open to them which led to the goal either of national honour or of national security.

No man has had to undertake a greater burden than the Prime Minister, who is our principal guest to-night. Let us be under no delusions. No man, in the months that lie in front of us, in that very arduous road which still remains to be trodden, carries a heavier responsibility than the Prime Minister. It has never been the habit of our countrymen in times of great crises to disparage the efforts of those on whom by universal admission we rely, and must continue to rely. For twelve months the Prime Minister of this country has been recognised among all our Allies as a man who held aloft the flaming and unquenchable torch of truth and courage. And if ever there was a tendency to lag in any one of our Allies, there is not one of us who will not admit that the note of hope and courage has come throughout from the man who has faced sufficient disasters, and sufficient threats of disasters, to quell the courage of the most valiant.

Turning to the Prime Minister, the Treasurer proceeded: We are here to-night to assure you that we to-day, at a moment when democracy stands in the scales in the sense that history will determine whether democracy as a machine for the purpose of waging efficient war is superior or inferior to autocracy—we are here at that critical moment to tell you that in our judgment the fortunes of democracy in this country and in this Empire rest in your hands. We give you also our support for what it is worth, and hope that when you appeal to your countrymen in this crisis, whatever be the demands that you think the necessities of the time require, we hope you will meet with the same response that the country has ever given to great and brave men. We do not say that the Government has not made mistakes. If anybody makes that shallow criticism we reply by saying, produce before us the Government which, faced by these novel and intractable problems, shaken by a cataclysm of events which defy any parallel—show us the Government which has not made errors, show us the General Staff which has not made errors. It is the experience of all countries that errors are made in such circumstances. It is happily the experience of ours above all others that our Government have developed in our history qualities of resolution, of endeavour, of imagination and resource which have risen victoriously above the consequences of their mistakes. And I say to you, as I am sure I may as the mouthpiece of those who are here to-night, that we have observed the devotion with which you have thrown yourself into this great task since you assumed it. We observed that you allowed yourself no leisure and no recreation; we observed that in exhausting weeks you have rushed to a conference in Paris, and a conference in Rome, and we have noted that wherever you have gone courage has been strengthened and resolution confirmed, so that to-day it is recognised, of yourself as of that great and distinguished statesman, President Wilson, that you hold in an unfaltering grip that torch of Anglo-Saxon freedom which shall assuredly one day most utterly destroy the fierce tyranny of Prussia.

We welcome, too, the Italian Ambassador. The representative of a chivalrous race, let him be sure that we realise to-day the great glory which has been won by the arms of Italy. I assure him, on your behalf, of the sympathy and admiration of this country for the Italian Army, and I tell him that we stand together in bad times, as we have stood together in good times, comrades and brothers.

The second object of our dinner is to mark and place on record our appreciation of that great consolidation of our Flying Services which has produced the new Air Force. We have present men who in almost every department have made that Service. We have representatives of the Navy, the Army, and the great manufacturers. Let me say, in conclusion, that in this historic hall, in which it is said Queen Elizabeth heard a play of Shakespeare at its first performance—the only hall in England, I believe, in which any play of Shakespeare was first produced; in this hall, in which Bacon lived and dreamed and wrote, and to which, like a wounded animal, he crept after his disgrace, to die among friends who never betrayed him; in this hall, in which Cromwell must surely have dined, I assure you, sir (the Premier), that the country of Bacon and Cromwell and Queen Elizabeth is the same England still, and is with you to-night, and in the searching and most grave months which lie in front of you.

THE PRIME MINISTER, who received an ovation on rising to reply, said: Your Excellencies, my Lords and Gentlemen. I must crave your indulgence to-night, as I have a good deal to say to you, and through you to the nation, in this crisis of our national fate. Before I do so, I should like to express my thanks for the honour you have conferred upon me in asking me to join such distinguished company in this historic building in meeting and greeting the representatives of the most romantic Service in this War. In the House of Commons I gave what I fear must be regarded as inadequate expression to the gratitude and admiration which the nation feels for this gallant Service. I have sometimes felt that the operations of the Air Service will probably have greater effect in determining the nations that this must be the last war than any other weapons however terrible their effect. They bring home to the people, who in former wars have dwelt in security, something of the perils and the horrors of the battlefield; and as the War goes on these will spread and increase and intensify. These winged messengers of death may therefore well become angels of peace. But we must also remember that whilst all that is true, they also give a greater significance and permanence to either victory or defeat. For however unjust or oppressive the conditions of any peace may be, the new terror added to war by this new weapon of dismay will create an intense and increased reluctance on the part of the world to challenge the issue anew. It is therefore more important than ever that the peace we secure shall be a just and an honourable and a beneficent peace.

Recently a highly respected nobleman, who has rendered distinguished service to the State in many spheres of activity, startled the nation by a letter which gave rise to very considerable apprehension on the part of those whose main anxiety is that this War should terminate in an upright and honourable and enduring peace, and not in a humiliating surrender. I now understand that all our anxieties as to this epistle were groundless; that Lord Lansdowne had not intended in the least to convey the meaning which was placed upon his words; that all the time he was in complete agreement with President Wilson, and that he was endeavouring to give expression to the same sentiments as the President of the United States uttered in the great speech which he delivered to Congress a few days ago. Now the Government are in full agreement with that speech, and I am not in the least surprised to find that Mr. Asquith is also in agreement with it. The British nation is undoubtedly in agreement with it, and as Lord Lansdowne has also declared that he agrees with it, things which agree with the same thing agree with one another. I therefore take it that the interpretation placed upon Lord Lansdowne's letter, not merely by strong supporters of the Allied cause, but also by its opponents in this country, in America and in France, and also I observe now also in Germany and in Austria, was not in the least that which Lord Lansdowne desired to give to it. I do not desire to force a controversy if none exists, for national unity is essential to success. But I may be forgiven for saying that if he intended to say the same thing as President Wilson, it is a great misfortune that he did not carry out that intention. I was attending the Allied Conference in Paris at the time that his letter appeared. It was received there with painful amazement. However, it is satisfactory to know that Lord Lansdowne was misunderstood both by his friends and by his critics, and that the whole weight of his great authority and influence may be reckoned on the side of the enforcement of what I call the Wilson policy.

I shall therefore pass on from this letter to the view which it was supposed to advocate, but did not, to the opinions which are held and expressed by a number of people in this country. It is true they are in a minority, but they are a very active minority, and they busy themselves insidiously, persistently, skilfully, impressing these views upon the people. The Lansdowne letter had the advantage of bringing them out into the open. They thought that at last they had discovered a leader, and there is no doubt that they were prepared to take action with a view to forcing this country into a premature and vanquished peace. The danger is not the extreme pacifist; I am not afraid of him. But I warn the nation to watch the man, whoever he is and wherever he comes from, who thinks there is a halfway house between victory and defeat. There is no halfway house between victory and defeat. These are the men who think that you can end the War now by some sort of what they call a pact of peace, by the mere setting up of a League of Nations with conditions as to arbitration in the event of disputes, with provision for disarmament and with a solemn covenant on the part of all nations to sign a treaty on these lines, and not merely to abide by it themselves, but help to enforce it against any nation that dares to break it. That is the right policy after victory. Without victory it would be a farce. Why, we are engaged in a war because an equally solemn treaty was treated as a scrap of paper. Who would sign the new Treaty? I presume amongst others the people who have so far successfully broken the last. Who would enforce the new Treaty? I presume they would be the nations that have so far not quite succeeded in enforcing the last. To end the war entered upon in order to enforce a Treaty without reparation for the infringement of that Treaty, merely by entering into a new and a more sweeping and a more comprehensive Treaty with the same people, would indeed be a farce in the setting of a tragedy. We must take care not to be misled by mere words—league of nations, disarmament, arbitration, security—they are all great and blessed phrases. But without the vitalising force of victory they are nothing but words, words, nothing but words. You cannot wage war with words. You cannot secure peace with words. You cannot long cover defeat with words. Unless there are deeds behind them, they are but dead leaves, which the first storm will scatter and reveal your strangled and abandoned purpose to the world.

We ought never to have started unless we meant at all hazards to complete our task. There is nothing so fatal to character as half-finished tasks. I can understand, although I cannot respect, the attitude of the men—and there are a few—who said from the first, "Do not interfere whatever happens." When you said to them, "Supposing the Prussians overrun Belgium?" their answer was, "Let them overrun Belgium." If you said, "We promised solemnly to protect Belgium against all invaders, and we ought to stand by our word," they reply, "We ought never to have given our word." If you said to them, "What if the Germans trample in the mire our friends and neighbours, the free Republic of France?" they answer, "That is not our business." If you ask, "What if they murder innocent people, old and young, male and female, burn cities and ravage and outrage before your eyes," in effect they said, "Let them perpetrate every crime in the calendar so long as it is not done in our land. What concern is it of ours? Are we our brothers' keepers? Let us not meddle and provoke anger which might disturb our serenity and our comfort." In fact, as one leading journalist put it with shameless candour, "Let us rather profit by manufacturing goods for both sides, for the assassins as well as for the survivors, amongst our friends." That is not an exalted line to take, but it is a definite and clear line of action, intelligible in consciences of a certain quality. "Ourselves first, ourselves last, ourselves all the time, and ourselves alone." It is pretty mean, but there are in every country men built that way, and we must reckon with them in the world. But the man I cannot comprehend is the sort of man, who, when he first saw these outrages, his generous soul was aflame with righteous wrath, and he called out, "In the name of Heaven let us leap in and arrest this infamy, and if we fail, then at least let us punish the perpetrators so as to make it impossible for it to happen again." And having said all this, and having helped to commit the nation to that career of honour, now, before the task is nearly accomplished, he suddenly turns round and says, "I have had enough of this. It is time it should come to an end. Let us shake hands with the malefactor. Let us trade with him to our mutual advantage." He is not to be asked for reparation for damage done. He need not even apologise. He is simply invited to enter into a bargain to join with you in punching the head of the next man who dares to imitate his villainies. And we are told we can have peace now on those terms. Germany has said so; Austria has said so; the Turk has said so. It must therefore be true. Of course it is true. Why should they refuse peace on such terms, especially as it would leave them with some of the richest provinces and fairest cities of Russia in their pockets? There are distinguished judges present. They are often called upon to administer justice for offences not unlike those committed by Prussia. It is true that rarely have they had before them a criminal who in his own person has committed all those offences—murder, arson, rape, burglary, fraud, piracy. Supposing next time they tried such a case and they are tired out by the insistence of the prisoner's advocate they were to turn round to the offender and say, "This is a profitless business. We are wasting a good deal of money and valuable time. I am weary of it. I want to get back to more useful work. If I let you off now without any punishment beyond that which is necessarily entailed in the expenses you have been put to in defending your honour, will you promise me to help the police to catch the next burglar? If you agree to these terms I propose to enrol you now as a Special Constable. I will now formally put on your armlet, and by the way, if you leave me your address I will promise, in order to cement the good feeling which I wish to prevail in future between us, to deal at your store without further inquiry as to where or how you got the goods. I might add that you need not worry to return the stuff you stole from your next-door neighbour on your right as I understand he has withdrawn his claim to restoration." Now, what do you think would be the effect on crime? It is idle to talk of security to be won by such feeble means. There is no security in any land without certainty of punishment. There is no protection for life, property or money in a State where the criminal is more powerful than the law. The law of nations is no exception, and until it has been vindicated the peace of the world will be always at the mercy of any nation whose professors have assiduously taught it to believe that no crime is wrong so long as it leads to the aggrandisement and enrichment of the country to which they owe allegiance. There have been many times in the history of the world criminal States. We are dealing with one of them now. And there will always be criminal States, until the reward of international crime becomes too precarious to make it profitable, and the punishment of international crime becomes too sure to make it attractive. Let there be no doubt as to the alternatives with which we are confronted. One of them is to make easy terms with the triumphant outlaw as men are driven to in order to buy immunity in lands where there is no authority to enforce law. That is one course. It means abasing ourselves in terror before lawlessness. It means ultimately a world intimidated by successful bandits. The other is to go through with our divine task of vindicating justice so as to establish a righteous and everlasting peace for ourselves and for our children, and for our children's children. Surely no nation with any regard for its interests, for its self-respect, for its honour, can hesitate for a moment in its choice between those two courses.

Victory is an essential condition for the security of a free world. All the same, intensely as I realise that, if I thought things would get no better the longer you fought, not merely would there be no object in prolonging the War, to do so would be infamous. To wantonly sacrifice brave lives, nay to force brave men to endure for one profitless hour the terrible conditions of this War merely because statesmen had not the courage to face the obloquy which would be involved in agreeing to an unsatisfactory peace, would be a black crime when we remember what we owe to those gallant men. It is because I am firmly convinced that despite some untoward events, despite discouraging appearances, we are making steady progress towards the goal we set in front of us in 1914, that I would regard peace overtures to Prussia at the very moment when the Prussian military spirit is drunk with boastfulness as a betrayal of the great trust with which my colleagues and I have been charged. Much of the progress we are making may not be visible except to those whose business it is to search out the facts. The victories of Germany are all blazoned forth to the world. Her troubles appear in no Press communiques or wireless messages, but we know something of these. The deadly grip of the British Navy is having its effect, and the indomitable valour, the undying valour, of our brave army is making an impression which in the end will tell. We are laying surely the foundation of the bridge which when it is complete will carry us across to the new world. The river is for the moment in spate and some of the scaffolding has been carried away, and much of the progress we had made seems to be submerged and hidden. And there are men who say, " Let us abandon the enterprise altogether. It is too costly. It is impracticable of achievement. Let us rather build a pontoon bridge of new treaties, league of nations, understandings." It might last you some time. It would always be shaky and uncertain. It would not bear much strain. It would not carry heavy traffic, and the first flood would sweep it away. Let us get along with the pile-driving and make a real, solid, permanent structure.

Meanwhile, let us maintain our steadiness and sanity of outlook. There are people who are too apt at one moment to get unduly elated at victories which are but incidents in the great march of events, and the same people get unwholesomely depressed by defeats which again are nothing more than incidents. The very persons who within the last fortnight have been organising a nervous breakdown in the nation, some weeks ago were organising an hysterical shout over our victories in Flanders and at Cambrai. We were breaking through the enemy's barrier; we were rolling up the German armies and clearing them out of Belgium and the North of France. They remind me of a clock I used to pass at one time of my life almost every day. It worried me a great deal; the works were out of order, for whatever the time of day, the fingers always pointed at twelve o'clock. If you trusted that clock you would have believed it was either noon or midnight. There are people of this type in this War, who one moment point to the high noon of triumph, and the next to the blank midnight of defeat or despair. There is no twilight. There is no morning. They can claim a certain consistency, for they are always at twelve, but you will find that their mainspring in this War is out of repair. We must go through all the hours minute by minute, second by second, with a steady swing, and if we do this, in God's own time the hour of dawn will strike.

This is not the most propitious hour. Why pretend it! Russia threatens to retire out of the War and leave the French democracy, whose loyalty to the word they passed to Russia brought upon them the horrors of this War, to shift for themselves with the aid of the Allies who mean to stick to their bond. I do not wish to minimise in the least the gravity of that decision. Had Russia been in a condition to exert her strength this year we might now be in a position to impose fair and rational terms of peace. By her retirement she strengthens Hohenzollernism and weakens the forces of democracy throughout the world. Her action will not lead as she imagines to universal peace. It will simply prolong the agony of the world, and it will inevitably put her in bondage to the military dominance of Prussia. But if Russia persists in her present policy, then the withdrawal from the Eastern flank of the enemy of forces which have hitherto absorbed over a third of his strength, must release hundreds of thousands of his troops and masses of material to attack Britain, France and Italy, before America arrives. It is a serious addition to our task which was already formidable enough. It would be folly to underrate the danger; it would be equal folly, on the other hand, to exaggerate it; the greatest folly of all would be not to face the danger. If the Russian democracy have decided to abandon the struggle against military autocracy, the American democracy is taking it up. That is the most momentous fact of this year. It has transposed the whole situation. The Russians are a great-hearted people, and valiantly have they fought in this War. But let me be quite candid with our friends. They have always been—certainly throughout this War—the worst organised State in Europe, and Britain with but a third of the population of Russia has been for the last two years a more formidable military antagonist to Germany. And had you asked Germany, not now, but even a year ago, which country she would prefer to see out of the War, I do not think there would have been any doubt about her answer.

But what about America? There is no more powerful country in the world than the United States of America, with their gigantic resources and their indomitable people; and if Russia is out, America is coming in with both arms. If this is the worst moment it is because Russia has stepped out and America is only preparing to come in. Her army is not ready; her equipment is not complete; her tonnage has not been built. Every hour that passes, the gap formed by the retirement of the Russians will be filled by the valiant sons of the great American Republic. Soon it will be more than filled. Germany knows it, Austria knows it—hence the desperate efforts they are making to force the issue before America is ready. They will not succeed. All the same, these two unfortunate circumstances, the collapse of Russia and the temporary defeat of Italy, undoubtedly cast upon us a heavier share of the burden until the strength of America is ready to come underneath to share it. We must therefore be prepared for greater efforts, for greater sacrifices. It is not the time to cower, to falter or to hesitate. It is the time for the nation to plant its feet more firmly than ever on the ground, and to square its shoulders to bear the increased weight cast upon it by events. When I talk of the nation I do not mean the nation in the abstract, but the millions of individuals who constitute the nation. If we are to win the security which it is the common purpose of all sections to attain, then every man and every woman must be prepared for greater endeavours and greater sacrifices. A friend of mine, speaking the other day, said there was not the enthusiasm observable which characterised the early days of the War. That may be so. If a man undertakes a long, arduous and perilous journey, you do not expect him in the fatiguing hours of the afternoon to exhibit the same ardour as when he started in the freshness of the morning. But although he may not display the same keenness in his demeanour, if he is a man of any purpose his ardour may be less but his resolution is greater. There is a hot zeal and a cold zeal, and the greatest things of the world have been accomplished by the latter. The will of Britain is as tempered steel. There is no sign of a break in it, and although the pressure may increase, and will increase, I have never doubted that it will bear it all right to the end. We shall have to call upon the nation for further sacrifice, but we shall only do so because it is absolutely necessary now. Premature sacrifice is waste of morale. There must be a further drain upon our man-power in order to sustain, until the American army arrives, the additional burden cast upon us by the defection of Russia and the reverses of Italy. We must have enough men to defend the lines we have held against fierce onsets for three years, and to defend them against all-comers from any quarter of the enemy front. We must also have an army of manœuvre which will enable us to appear with the least delay at any point of emergency in any part of the colossal battlefield. There is no ground for panic. Even now after we have sent troops to the assistance of Italy, the Allies have a marked superiority of numbers in France and Flanders and we have considerable reserves at home. Much greater progress has been made in man-power, especially during the last few months, than either friends or foes realise, but it is not enough in order to enable us to face contingencies without anxiety unless we take further steps to increase our reserves of trained men.

Before I leave this branch of the subject I must, however, add another important consideration. While the Cabinet are prepared with recommendations for raising more men, they are conducting a searching investigation, with the assistance of our military advisers, into the best methods of husbanding the man-power already existing in our armies so as to reduce the terrible wastage of war. But the problem of man-power does not end with the provision of men for the armies. It is not even the most urgent part of the problem. We need more men not merely for the battle-line across the seas, but for the battle-line in this country. We especially need men to help us to solve the problems associated with tonnage. You can increase tonnage in two ways—by building tonnage and by saving tonnage. Victory is now a question of tonnage, and tonnage is victory. Nothing else can defeat us now but shortage of tonnage. The advent of the United States into the War has increased the demand enormously. Tonnage must be provided for the transportation of that gigantic new army which they are raising with its equipment across thousands of miles of sea. It is no use raising ten million men and equipping them, and it is no use building endless aeroplanes unless you get them somewhere in the vicinity of the foe. Germany has gambled on America's failure to transport her army to Europe, and that is why she is still laughing at the colossal figures of soldiers in training, and aeroplanes in course of construction. We know that the Prussian War Lords have promised their own people, have promised their Allies, that these formidable masses will never find their way into the battle-line, and that President Wilson's speeches, Monsieur Clemenceau's speeches, and my poor speeches will be added to the vast collection of unredeemed rhetoric with which, according to them, democracies have always deluded themselves. The Prussian claim is that autocracy alone can do these things, and that democracies can only talk of doing these things. The honour of democracy is at stake. I have no doubt that here, as in many other respects, those who trust the Prussians will be disillusioned, but both America and ourselves will have to strain our resources to the utmost in order to increase the tonnage available. The fact that American tonnage will be absorbed in the transport of their own army makes it necessary that we should increase our responsibilities in the matter of assisting our French and our Italian allies to transport essential commodities to their shores. We must therefore increase our tonnage. In spite of the fact that we have had less labour available in this country in this the fourth year of the War than we have ever had before, we have increased the shipbuilding of war and merchant vessels beyond the record of any other war years and, as Sir Eric Geddes stated in the House of Commons, we are now turning out ships at a rate which is above that of the record year of shipbuilding in the days of peace. But we must do more. As the whole future of this country and of the world depends upon the efforts Britain and America make this next year to increase the output of ships, we are resolved that it must and shall be done.

But we must have men; and in order to have men we must interfere even to a greater extent than we have done already with the industries which are not absolutely essential for the prosecution of the War, or to the maintenance of the life of the nation. And however great the hardships that may be inflicted by this interference upon the particular trades involved, we must ask the nation to support us. And I feel certain that the trades themselves will show that patriotism which has characterised every section of the community in this great national endeavour.

I would only add one further word about shipping. As I have already pointed out, you can increase tonnage in two ways—by building tonnage, and by saving tonnage. I have dealt with the first. I will say a word about the second. You save tonnage by economising—economising in food, economising in dress. You save tonnage by increasing the production in this country of material formerly imported from abroad—food, timber, minerals. All this involves additional labour. As to food, this year we increased the home production by two or three million tons. We are the only belligerents who have succeeded in increasing our food output during the War, and great credit is due to those who by a superb feat of organisation and inspiration have achieved this result. But it is essential that we should still further increase the home supplies. We must save another three million tons in our food imports next year. This means that all those who have land either as owners or cultivators must help us, must without delay show their readiness to fall in with plans for increasing the produce of the land. We shall do our best to provide the necessary labour and machinery and I am confident we shall succeed, but all prejudice, all predilections must be swept aside. The nation must be saved; victory must come first. Two or three million tons more food raised in this country means two or three millions tons of shipping made available for strengthening the armies in the field. Every ton of food you produce in this country is an increased weight hurled against the Prussian barrier. The nation can help by giving up the things which are not essential to victory. We must strip even barer for the fight. The nation can help in another way—by discouraging grousers. Grousing undermines morale, and when it is a question of holding out the national morale is vital. You cannot expect things to go on smoothly in war as they do in peace. You can realise how much the ordinary life of the nation has been disturbed by the simple transposition of the figures of our War Budget into terms of the amount of national energy which its huge sums are intended to purchase. You cannot take millions of men away from the tasks of supplying the peace needs of the community without seriously interfering with the comforts and amenities of life of that community. The wonder is that the disturbance has not been greater, and I feel we owe much gratitude to the experienced and able business men who, in various directions, have undertaken to organise the resources of the State for war, for the services they have rendered not merely in increasing our efficiency for war, but in minimising the evils and inconveniences of war. It is a remarkable fact that, although our imports have enormously diminished, there is less hunger in the land to-day than in August, 1914. I ask you to help these men and not to rattle them. The strain upon them is enormous. Make their task easier. There are some people engaged in a constant and systematic grumble. The peace propaganda is fed with grumbles. These people are anxious to break down the national nerve, and then rush us into a premature and disastrous peace. Let us beware of playing their game.

We have challenged a sinister power which is menacing the world with enslavement. It would have been better never to have issued the challenge unless you meant to carry it through. A challenged Power which is not overthrown always becomes stronger for the challenge. The people who think they can begin a new era of peace whilst the Prussian military power is unbeaten are labouring under a strange delusion. We have all been dreaming of a new world to appear when the deluge of war has subsided. Unless we achieve victory for the great cause for which we entered this War, the new world will simply be the old world with the heart out of it. The old world at least believed in ideals. It believed that justice, fair play, liberty, righteousness must triumph in the end. That is, however you interpret the phrase, the old world believed in God, and it staked its existence on that belief. Millions of gallant young men volunteered to die for that Divine faith. But if wrong emerged triumphant out of this conflict, the new world would feel in its soul that brute force alone counted in the government of man, and the hopelessness of the dark ages would once more fall on the earth like a cloud. To redeem Britain—to redeem Europe—to redeem the world from this doom must be the settled purpose of every man and woman who places duty above ease. This is the fateful hour of mankind. If we are worthy of the destiny with which it is charged, untold generations of men will arise to thank God for the strength He gave us to endure to the end.

The Treasurer in proposing the toast of the "Air Force," said: Mr. Junior, my Lords and Gentlemen. I indicated before the extremely important and interesting speech which the Prime Minister has delivered that our dinner to-night had two purposes. The first was to assure him, as we have assured him, of our support, and I think he will leave us to-night with the knowledge of that support; and the second was to propose the health and the prosperity of the Air Service. We have here to-night a great number of men who are entitled to the most distinguished consideration for the services which they have rendered in the gradual process of the conquest of the air. We have here high representatives of the Admiralty and the Army, and equally important, we have representative manufacturers; and it is in the co-ordination of the efforts of them all that the secret of the supremacy of the air is to be found. How strange it would have appeared some ten years ago if any one had hazarded the prediction that the future of the world war might be determined by the conquest of the air. It may well be that in the next twelve months the future of the War will be determined by that conquest. And when we think of the matchless powers of improvisation to which this great nation has proved itself equal in the last three years, we must recognise that none has been more amazing than its progress in the subjugation of the air.

We have here many who have differed in their views of the necessities of the time. We have present, for instance, Mr. Joynson Hicks. I remember him as an old critic who long before the War declared that there was an immense military future in the air, and that our provisions in that direction were inadequate. The War has proved him to be right. We have here also, and if I may say so, an interesting and an arresting personality, one of the most brilliant members of the House of Commons, a man who commands audiences which many Cabinet Ministers fail to secure. I refer to Lord Hugh Cecil, who, at the beginning of this War, qualified as a pilot, and has since rendered very great service in the organisation of the Flying Corps. Success can only be achieved by harmony and co-ordination among all those who are engaged in mastering the enemy in the air. If there is to be competition between the Army and the Navy and then a third element of competition by some neutral, or hermaphrodite Board, it is evident that there never can be success. But there can be success if all those concerned in the greatness of this country and the efficiency of our airmen can speak, not for one force or another force, but for England in the air.

What does it mean, the War in the air? It is very easy for us in the luxury and security of this Hall to assume the performances of our airmen, but I wonder if it is possible in imagination for those of us who have not been called upon to take part to conceive the efforts, the sacrifice and the gallantry of those young heroes—all boys—who go from the public schools to set a seal on the valour of this nation the like of which has never been known. We talk of the valour of the Homeric heroes, but the only clouds in which they fought were provided by the goddesses for their protection. The valour of the heroes of Homer, made musical by the praise of poets, has been far, far surpassed by that of our own airmen. Let there be no delusion. Never have the stamina and fibre of the human race been tried as it has been tried in the exertions which day by day the boys of the Air Services are making. Many of them had been living lives of luxury, and now these boys from Harrow, Eton and Oxford, and the grammar schools of the Empire, every day take their lives in their hands, and they do it for us.

The Air Service which this country has produced is the wonder and admiration of the world. We welcome to-night the new Secretary of State for the Air. We have here, too, the most distinguished soldiers and sailors, on whom we shall have to rely in the exercise of their official duties; and I venture to make myself their mouthpiece when I say that the great task which lies before him will not be complicated by any inter-Service jealousies. No Minister ever faced a more difficult task with more courage than my right honourable and noble friend whose toast we honour. His difficult task would be made more difficult, and even insurmountable, unless the Military and Naval Services determine that they will make his task easy. They will make up their minds that all the old things have ceased to count; and that there will be no controversy between the Army and the Navy.

The Army salutes the valour of the Navy, and the Navy is never tired of saluting the bravery of the infantry. Let us all realise this, and let this dinner be the sign and seal that both and all the Flying Services count for England, and that England may depend upon all. In this spirit and this hope I give you the toast of the Air Force.

THE AIR MINISTER (Lord Rothermere) replied as follows: Mr. Treasurer, my Lords and Gentlemen. I thank you sincerely for your cordial reception of the toast. In the creation of the new force you have thus honoured, a great work of consolidation and unification was called for. When, in succession to Lord Cowdray, I decided to " go over the top " with the Prime Minister and accepted the position of Air Minister, I did so with the full confidence that the two senior services, the Navy and Army, would extend ungrudging assistance and support to the new service, the Air Force, which is now being established. My brief experience of a fortnight has proved to me that my confidence has not been misplaced. I feel that instead of the rebuffs which some people prophesied, I shall, whenever I require assistance, find a helping hand extended to me both by the Navy and the Army. Without such assistance it would be impossible for any man to make a success of the position I hold.

It is no easy task to dissever the aerial branches of the Navy and the Army and weld them into one harmonious whole. It is a gigantic work of organisation. The Royal Naval Air Service and the Royal Flying Corps are two distinct bodies with different ranks, different rates of pay and different organisations.

My advisers have asked me to be precise in my statement of our air policy. Much talk only encourages the enemy and is apt to discourage our people at home. In this statement there comes first and foremost the question of reprisals. At the Air Board we are wholeheartedly in favour of reprisals. It is our duty to avenge the murder of innocent women and children. As the enemy elect, so it will be the case of " an eye for an eye and a tooth for a tooth," and in this respect we shall strive for complete and satisfying retaliation.

General Ludendorff proclaims the present war a war of nations, suggesting that the civilian population is as much a mark for the airman's bombs as the fighting men. We detest this doctrine, holding it to be grossly immoral. But, fighting for our lives and for the lives of our women and children, we will not consent to its one-sided application. We have too much at stake in this contest to concede any advantage to a treacherous enemy. He has to learn in this, as in larger things, that it does not pay. We are determined, in other words, that whatever outrages are committed on the civilian population of this country will be met by similar treatment to his own people. The great asset of the Flying Services is the young Britisher, whether born in these islands or in the Dominions overseas. He makes the ideal fighter: he has courage, daring and heaps of initiative. Our duty is to see that he obtains all that he wants. My brief experience teaches me that the production of aircraft in great numbers is not the easy task that many people imagine. If the aeroplane had reached its ultimate development the task would not be anything like so difficult, but hardly a moment passes without some step, very often a great step, being made in the improvement of the aeroplane. The output of machines has increased in a most satisfactory way, and I have no doubt that at the present rate of progress it will not be long before the many criticisms which have been levelled at the Air Ministry are silenced.

For the rest, I am reminded by this gathering in so famous a place that the greatest of your treasurers, Lord Chancellor Bacon, has perhaps given an Air Minister to-day the best advice that he can gain from the wisdom of the ancients. "The condition of weapons and their improvement," he says in his famous essay "Of the Vicissitude of Things," "are first the fetching afar off." And what hits or fetches farther off than an aeroplane? "Next, the strength of the percussion, and, third, the commodious use of all weapons, as that they may serve in all weathers, that the carriage may be light and manageable and the like." Here, if I need it, the great ghost of Gray's Inn gives me not only inspiration but actually sound advice. My coming here to-day has served to remind me of it.

Commodore Godfrey Paine, C.B., M.V.O., and General Sir David Henderson, K.C.B., also replied to the toast.

THE TREASURER: My Lords and Gentlemen. I now give you the health of "The Flying Officers," and I couple with it the names of Lieutenant-Colonel Scott and Commander Butler. Colonel Scott—and I can speak with knowledge—specialised in this branch in the early days of the War, when he left the Yeomanry and joined the Royal Flying Corps because he saw the possibilities of aviation. In the first five months of the War he had an accident with an aeroplane and brought it down about 3000 feet, with the result that both his legs were smashed. He was lucky to escape with his life. Under those circumstances he was appointed to the staff of the Air Service. After serving on the staff for six months he was passed for foreign service. He went to France, and in the short period of seven months he made the reputation of being one of the bravest men in the British Army. A former barrister, he is now a Lieutenant-Colonel to whose name every man in the Flying Corps would pay tribute. Our airmen have rendered great and gallant service in this War, and with every confidence I ask you to drink to the health of the Flying Officers, coupled with the names of Lieutenant-Colonel Scott and Commander Butler.

Lieutenant-Colonel Scott and Commander Butler briefly replied.

THE TREASURER: My Lords and Gentlemen. I feel we should be lacking if we parted to-night without proposing a toast which is traditional here, and I therefore give you "The Bench of England." We all of us owe a great deal to the Bench. The impartiality with which their decisions are given in every crisis is a priceless asset to the nation. We have many great Judges here whose names will long be preserved in our legal literature. But we have one here whom it is especially fitting that we should honour. There is only one man who ought to reply in England to the toast of "The Bench," and that is the venerable Lord Halsbury. We are proud of him. He has lived for ninety-six years. He has spent his life all day long imbibing microbes in the Law Courts, and all night long imbibing further microbes in the House of Commons. He has toiled in such atmospheres while others have been deer-stalking or hunting, and here he is, hale and hearty before us, while his contemporaries, even the strongest of them, have long since been gathered to their fathers. He is the very type of the fibre and the stamina of our race.

Charge your glasses then, gentlemen, and drink a bumper to the nestor of the British Bench—to the sagacious and venerable Lord Halsbury.

Lord Halsbury: My Lords and Gentlemen. Some of you may have in your minds the impression that it would be as well if, among the various regulations which have been passed, there had been an arrangement by which the number of speeches were regulated, much in the way that food is now controlled. I recognise with gratitude, as I think we all do, the statements we have heard that we have a Government now in power which is not ashamed to own that it will do the right because it is the right. While in Courts of Law we have been obliged to have recourse to a certain amount of evidence, we all recognise that a man who does not keep his bargain is a scoundrel. The only reason why we insist in certain cases on a written document, such as a "scrap of paper," is because there are some people who are rogues and will disown what they have agreed to do. For that reason we are compelled in the Courts of Law to insist upon certain evidence that such and such a bargain has been made. But, so far as I know, in the history of mankind it has been a recognised fact that once a bargain is made it should be kept. Whatever we have heard to-night, nothing has shaken our confidence in the faith that what we have agreed to do we will do, whatever may be the result. I have very little to say, and perhaps for that reason you will be the more grateful to me. But I have one thing to say in which I am sure we all will acquiesce, and that is that we have a Treasurer who has been good enough to give us to-night a great entertainment, and I have to propose that we should all drink his health.

We are glad to have had such an utterance as we have heard from the Prime Minister—an open exposition of what we mean and an assurance of our determination that what we mean we will certainly do. The man who does what is right whatever may be the result of what he does, is certainly a man whom we should approve as a Minister of State. On the other hand, the man who departs from what he has agreed to do is not only a dirty scoundrel, but a man who deserves the utter detestation and condemnation of every person in the world, whether he wears a ragged jacket or the crown of an Empire.

The toast was accorded musical honours, the company singing " For he's a jolly good fellow."

THE TREASURER, in reply, said: I thank you all for the kindness with which you have received the toast, proposed by Lord Halsbury, with a vigour which is refreshing to all our hearts. I can only say that this Inn of which I have the honour of being Treasurer, is an Inn which has played a great and worthy part in the history of this country. It is an Inn which Queen Elizabeth visited, and we still have the chair which she presented to the Inn. We also still have the table from which she dined, which was formed from timbers captured from the Spanish Armada. And of this I am sure, that no surroundings could have been found more appropriate for the Prime Minister to deliver the great patriotic speech he has given than those of this Inn. There is no political controversy here to-night. We are proud that the Prime Minister, at the crisis in this War, chose this historic Hall as the scene of the message he has delivered to this Empire. I am sure this country and this Empire will not fall short of the Prime Minister's exhortation. Under his inspiration every citizen in his several part will struggle ever more strenuously until victory is finally won.

The memorable proceedings closed with the singing of the National Anthem.

Henry Dixon & Son, London, Photogravure.

Gray's Inn Gardens—"The London Welsh"—At Physical Drill in 1915.

JULY 29th, 1918.

The dinner to the Ministers responsible for the Fighting Forces of the Crown in Gray's Inn Hall on the 29th of July, 1918, *was held under happier circumstances than the previous gathering of the 14th of December,* 1917.

Though not at the time recognised by all, the turning point of the War had been reached. The fierce German offensive of the Spring had spent its fury. The second battle of the Marne had been fought and won. We were on the eve of the great British Victory of the 8th of August, 1918, *which General Ludendorff has described as "The black day of the German Army in the history of this War." And the United States was now coming with irresistible force into the War.*

It is not surprising, therefore, that a vein of cheerful confidence runs through the speeches in contrast with the more sombre note which pervaded the proceedings on the earlier night when the fate of the Empire seemed to hang in an uncertain balance.

SPEECHES

AT A DINNER GIVEN TO THE MINISTERS RESPONSIBLE FOR THE FIGHTING FORCES OF THE CROWN IN GRAY'S INN HALL ON MONDAY, THE 29th OF JULY, 1918.

The Treasurer (the Right Hon. Sir Frederick Smith, Bart., K.C., M.P., Attorney-General) presided.

The Company present included:

The Right Hon. Earl Curzon of Kedleston, G.C.S.I., G.C.I.E.; the Right Hon. G. N. Barnes, M.P.; General the Right Hon. J. C. Smuts, K.C.; the Right Hon. Austen Chamberlain, M.P. (*Members of the War Cabinet*).

The Lord Chancellor (the Right Hon. Lord Finlay, G.C.M.G.); the Right Hon. Sir Robert Borden, G.C.M.G. (Prime Minister of Canada); the Home Secretary (the Right Hon. Sir George Cave, K.C., M.P.); the Secretary for War (the Right Hon. Viscount Milner, G.C.B.); the First Lord of the Admiralty (the Right Hon. Sir Eric Geddes, K.C.B., M.P.); the Air Minister (the Right Hon. Lord Weir); the Colonial Secretary (the Right Hon. Walter Long, M.P.); the Minister of Munitions (the Right Hon. Winston Churchill, M.P.); the President of the Local Government Board (the Right Hon. W. Hayes Fisher, M.P.); the President of the Board of Education (the Right Hon. H. A. L. Fisher, M.P.); the Minister of Labour (the Right Hon. G. H. Roberts, M.P.); the Minister of Pensions (the Right Hon. John Hodge, M.P.); the Shipping Controller (the Right Hon. Sir Joseph Maclay); the Minister of National Service (the Right Hon. Sir Auckland Geddes, K.C.B.); the Minister of Reconstruction (the Right Hon. Christopher Addison, M.P.); the Minister of Blockade (Sir L. Worthington Evans, Bart., M.P.); the Postmaster-General (the Right Hon. A. H. Illingworth, M.P.); the Lord Privy

Seal (the Right Hon. the Earl of Crawford); the Chancellor of the Duchy of Lancaster (the Right Hon. Lord Beaverbrook); the Solicitor-General (Sir Gordon Hewart, K.C., M.P.); the Lord Advocate for Scotland (the Right Hon. J. A. Clyde, K.C., M.P.); the Deputy Minister of Munitions (Major-General the Right Hon. J. E. B. Seely, C.B., D.S.O., M.P.); the Under-Secretary of the Air Ministry (Major J. L. Baird, D.S.O., M.P.); the Parliamentary Secretary of the Ministry of Munitions (Mr. F. G. Kellaway, M.P.); General Sir Henry Wilson, K.C.B. (Chief of the Imperial General Staff); Admiral Sir Rosslyn Wemyss, K.C.B. (First Sea Lord); Rear-Admiral Sir W. R. Hall, K.C.B. (Director of Naval Intelligence); General Sir John Cowans, K.C.B. (Quartermaster-General of the Forces); General Sir George Macdonogh, K.C.M.G., C.B. (Adjutant-General to the Forces); General F. H. Sykes, C.M.G. (Chief of the Air Staff); Brigadier-General R. M. Groves (Deputy Chief of the Air Staff).

The Right Hon. the Master of the Rolls (Sir Charles Swinfen Eady); the Right Hon. Lord Sumner; the President of the Probate, Divorce and Admiralty Division; the Right Hon. Lord Justice Pickford; the Right Hon. Mr. Justice Darling; the Hon. Mr. Justice Roche; Sir Richard Muir; His Honour Judge Tobin, K.C.; Mr. P. O. Lawrence, K.C.; Mr. E. Tindal Atkinson, K.C.; Mr. Harold Smith, M.P.; the President of the Law Society (Mr. R. A. Pinsent); Sir George Lewis, Bart.; Admiral Sims, G.C.M.G. (U.S.A. Navy); Major-General Sir Newton Moore, K.C.M.G. (G.O.C., Australian Forces, United Kingdom); Sir Robert Garran, C.M.G. (Solicitor-General for Australia); Mr. Franklin Roosevelt (Assistant-Secretary U.S.A. Navy); Mr. Paul Cravath; His Excellency the Italian Ambassador; His Grace the Duke of Marlborough; His Grace the Duke of Rutland; His Grace the Duke of Northumberland; Lord Ivor Spencer-Churchill; the Right Hon. Viscount Cowdray; Viscount Duncannon, M.P.; the Right Hon. Lord Burnham; Lieut.-Colonel Sir Mark Sykes, Bart., M.P.; Lieut.-Colonel Sir Mathew Wilson, D.S.O., M.P.; Sir Arthur Duckham, K.C.B.; Sir Leonard Llewelyn, K.C.B.; the Right Hon. A. Birrell, K.C., M.P.;

Captain the Hon. Frederick Guest, D.S.O., M.P.; Sir Reginald Brade, K.C.B.; Mr. H. J. Creedy, C.B.; Lieut.-Commander H. W. S. Chilcott; Mr. Edward Hulton; the Right Hon. Sir Edward Goulding, Bart., M.P.; Brigadier-General B. E. W. Childs, C.M.G.; Lieut.-Colonel C. L. Whitburn; Major W. A. Bishop, V.C., D.S.O., M.C.

The Masters of the Bench present, in addition to the Treasurer, were: Master Henry Goudy, D.C.L.; Master His Honour Judge Mulligan, K.C.; Master M. W. Mattinson, K.C.; Master Sir Lewis Coward, K.C.; Master C. A. Russell, K.C.; Master the Hon. Sir Montague Lush; Master T. Terrell, K.C.; Master W. T. Barnard, K.C.; Master the Right Hon. Lord Justice Duke; Master the Right Hon. Sir James Campbell, Bart. (Lord Chancellor of Ireland); Master H. F. Manisty, K.C.; Master Edward Clayton, K.C.; Master Arthur E. Gill; Master E. F. Vesey Knox, K.C.; Master the Right Hon. Sir William Byrne, K.C.V.O., C.B.; Master Montagu Sharpe, D.L.; Master F. A. Greer, K.C.; Master C. Herbert-Smith; Master Lieut.-Colonel His Honour Judge Ivor Bowen, K.C.; Master Sir Alexander Wood-Renton; Master R. E. Dummett; Master Colonel Sir Hamar Greenwood, Bart., M.P., with the Preacher (the Rev. R. J. Fletcher, D.D.) and the Under-Treasurer.

After the toasts of "The King," "The Queen, Queen Alexandra, the Prince of Wales and other Members of the Royal Family," "The Memory of Our Members who have fallen in the War," and "Domus."

THE TREASURER proposed "The War Cabinet." He said: Mr. Junior, your Excellency, my Lords and Gentlemen. During the War the activities of the Inns of Court in the sphere of their corporate activity have been largely suspended because the vitality of their youth and the experience of their age have been diverted to other fields. They have suspended their Grand Nights and those historic occasions of hospitality on which they pride themselves. We, too, have made these sacrifices owing to the circumstances of the time. We have, however, allowed ourselves on very rare occasions with pleasure to call to our ancient Hall the men who are playing a great part in the controversies of this day. To-night we have the honour, and we greatly value it, of welcoming the First Lord of the Admiralty and his Chief of Staff, the Secretary of State for War and his Chief of Staff, the Minister of the new Air Force and his Chief of Staff. We cannot welcome them on one side of our entertainment as we should have done five years ago, but we are not conscious of any lack of quality, we hope, on the liquid side of the refreshment to which we bid you hospitable welcome. We are fortunate in having among us many prominent representatives of our Allies. Englishmen, I think, have done all that is in their power to render adequate tribute to the services rendered by all our Allies in the cause of our common civilisation. When these things are looked at after four years of war they improve in perspective. England and America and all the Allies realise that had it not been for the military contribution, relatively small as it was, which we were able to make in the early days of the War, the whole fortunes of the Allies would have tottered to ruin at the first assault. France, too—and the world will never forget it—sacrificed the best of her youth in the cause of civilisation, and by so doing they saved that cause. She has to-day added to the burden of gratitude under which civilisation lies to her by her example of inspiration and of supreme strategical genius. We have been told by our enemies to recognise in them the masters of military art. We reply to that by saying, "You were the only nation which prepared for war. No nation in history ever enjoyed the opportunity of unrestricted organisation which was given to the self-appointed Napoleon of our day, and you are beaten at your own game." Let us give the meed of glory which the great French nation deserve at this moment of our triumph. They, and not the Germans, are the masters of the military art—an art as elusive, as incalculable and as intellectual as any which tests and taxes the resources of the human mind. And while we recognise the intellectual supremacy of the work of the French staff, we shall still make bold to claim that the British infantry, cheerful, stubborn, unconquerable, is still the finest military material in the world. And we welcome His Excellency the Italian Ambassador, the true friend of this country, and let me tell him in your name and mine that we shall never forget, nor will our children forget how the Italian nation pledged itself and all it stands for—pledged the glorious beauty of Venice—pledged it in the very darkest moment of the Allied Forces, when the Russian hosts were reeling under the German assaults—when all might have been lost in the East and before the gigantic republic of the West had found itself. All honour to our Allies who chose that moment to make a supreme effort and say, "We will bide by the issues which await civilisation, whatever the cost." Your country, sir, will rank high in the cool valuation of history for the part the Italian nation has played in this War, and I am certain that when those who busy themselves in recounting military achievements and the causes which affect and destroy the *morale* of soldiers complete their task, no more remarkable history will ever be written, none more glorious than the story of the resilience and military quality of your army—that which records how the Army, which met with disasters which saddened us, was able to restore and re-animate itself, and to pluck from a bloody discomfiture the sure and certain hope of an ultimate victory. We welcome your Excellency to-night as our honoured guest, and in honouring you as our guest, we honour the nation you represent.

And I add, not without emotion, an observation about our greatest Ally, the American nation. We are honoured by entertaining to-night the representatives of that nation, Admiral Sims, sitting, as he ought to sit, side by side with the First Lord of our Admiralty. He has proved himself, from the first moment he landed in this country, a great friend of England, and one who was destined to contribute a powerful part in the fostering of friendly feeling between his country and ours and in the consolidation of the maritime power of the Allies. To-night we also welcome, almost by accident, the member of a glorious family, Mr. Roosevelt, who is Assistant-Secretary of the American Navy. We are not concerned here with the domestic differences of American politics, but there is no one here, to whatever school of American politics he belongs, who will quarrel with me when I say that the distinguished head of that family is one of the greatest men ever produced by the American nation, and I venture to say that the words of sympathy he spoke with this country in its darkest days will not soon fade from the minds and memories of Englishmen. Members of that family have made great sacrifices in the War, and no one will welcome Mr. Roosevelt on his visit to England with a warmer hand and heart than we do. With regard to the War Cabinet, I do not claim the privilege of lecturing the War Cabinet. My duty to-night is not to lecture them but to propose their health, and I propose it with a very sincere feeling of sympathy and admiration. It is not for me to inquire whether the particular members of this Cabinet were or were not the best that could have been chosen. In the highest circles controversies upon such topics are not discouraged. But the fact remains that they have stood for England in these most critical years. I fully consider all the claims that may be made for the age of Chatham, but I say this (even challenging comparison with those spacious days), that, toiling by day and night, they have stood for England and the British Empire, and they have never weakened and never faltered. When I ask you to drink this toast, I ask you to drink the health of men who have listened for years to bitter and adverse criticism—very often the result of disappointment and sometimes of hysteria. Every one knows that this nation has gone through terrible times. Individuals, who after all in the aggregate make up the nation, men, women and children, have suffered great loss, and if some hysteria has made itself articulate and sometimes shrill, we must reduce it to the proper proportion in speaking of the whole nation. But this I venture to say, that the feeling of the English nation, and of the whole British Empire, is hardening every day against the Germans, and the War Cabinet has never wavered in the darkest moments in its confidence or its resolution. I think it is true, as Mr. Churchill said in an eloquent speech on Independence Day, that there is no peace possible which does not teach Germany that she is vanquished. I think the feeling of this Empire is growing more and more definite against any attempt in the direction of negotiations. And when I read what President Wilson said the other day—"Force to the uttermost"—I asked myself whether any even verbal distinction existed between this policy and that of our Prime Minister. And the policy of the Prime Minister and of the knock-out blow has been the policy of the War Cabinet. We realise all that they have done; and we are alive to their anxieties and responsibilities when we toast the War Cabinet. They have to consider, and no doubt they will consider, whether the Empire can afford to tolerate a new Heligoland in the Pacific. I desire to-night, speaking on your behalf in an assembly which primarily consists of lawyers, to make it plain that it is a great privilege to us to entertain many men who represent the fighting services. Lord Curzon is one who has played a very great part in the War, who came with the ripe experience of a Viceroy of India and was one of the first members of Mr. Asquith's Cabinet, who has been a member of the War Cabinet every since, and to whose industry and balanced judgment his colleagues will bear willing tribute. In raising our glasses we raise them to men who have rendered great services to the State, and who we believe will render still greater services to the State in years to come. Charge your glasses then, my Lords and Gentlemen, and drink to the health of the War Cabinet, which I associate with the name of Earl Curzon.

EARL CURZON, replying to the toast, said: I had always heard that the banquets in the ancient and tranquil Halls of the Inns of Court were occasions when the wicked cease from troubling and the weary are at rest, and when even a Cabinet Minister could enjoy the luxury of a convivial evening without either listening to others, or being obliged to ask others to listen to him. But these dreams were rudely shattered when your Treasurer informed me, two days ago, that he proposed to ignore this comfortable tradition and to propose the toast of "The War Cabinet," to which it would be my duty to respond. I had no alternative but to express unhesitating obedience to his commands. I am well aware that the toast is not personal to the present members of that body. We happen to be the persons who are charged, for the time being, with the management of the greatest War in which this country has ever been engaged. I am not so vain as to imagine that we do it better than any other people: indeed, we are almost daily informed, by some of our friends in the Press, that we do it worse. Only the other day the Prime Minister was appealed to by the leading organ of public opinion to discharge the passengers in the coach. When we read this admonition, my colleagues and I in the War Cabinet wondered which of us was likely to survive the test. As we looked around and measured the qualifications of our colleagues against our own, there may have occurred to us the famous dictum of Lord Justice Bowen, who, when it was proposed to commence an address from the judges to Queen Victoria on one of her Jubilees with the phrase, "Conscious as we are of our own imperfections," proposed, amid general agreement, to amend it as follows: "Conscious as we are of each other's imperfections!" A similar thought may perhaps have occurred on the present occasion to our minds.

I cannot help thinking, however, that, in answering to this toast, I am responding not for the War Cabinet only, but for the Imperial War Cabinet as well—several of whose members are seated at these tables. We have been in session with them for the best part of two months. They have brought to our deliberations the stimulus of a fresh and detached vision, the assurance of the unshaken fortitude of the free nations which they represent, and a reaffirmation of the great purpose for which we are fighting, and in the pursuance of which I agree with you, Mr. Treasurer, in holding that there can be no compromise, no weakening, no abatement. When the Imperial War Cabinet meets, it supersedes the War Cabinet, and becomes the supreme Executive of the Empire for all purposes of war. There is no information which they do not possess, no responsibility which they do not share. In these meetings there are some of us who see the germs of a great constitutional development and the key to some of the vexed Empire problems of the future. The War has altered many things: perhaps it may be found to have altered the Constitution itself. For years we have been talking about Imperial Federation, a closer Imperial union, and various methods of uniting for future action the British Empire. The War has come, and in a moment, in the twinkling of an eye, almost in a breath, it has carried us far forward on the road to solution. There is not one of us who doubts that the machinery which was devised for a couple of months in the year must assume a more permanent and less spasmodic shape. We want to consult the Dominion Ministers, and they want to be consulted by us, not for two months in the twelve, but for the whole of the year. They must continue to have a voice in the great decisions of the Council Chamber, as their armies have had in those of the field. I should be surprised and disappointed if, out of our War deliberations, there does not develop some organisation that will inure for peace. The materials are there, a commonwealth of free nations meeting on a footing of absolute equality, pooling their resources, sharing their sacrifices, and exerting their efforts to a common end. This great experiment in Imperial brotherhood cannot pass away without producing a change in the machinery that shall adjust itself to the facts. The constituents are already in existence. Who knows that the Constitution may not shortly follow?

I speak at a moment of great significance in the history of the War. I am not so foolish as to suggest that we are at the turning-point of the War; to say that would be to indulge in premature and foolish jubilation. But it is conceivable that the events of the last fortnight may be destined to exercise an influence on the whole course of the campaign not less remarkable than the original and famous Battle of the Marne four years ago. For what has passed? After their great successes in March, April and May, the enemy was in a position which constituted a serious menace equally to the Channel Ports, to the continued junction and co-operation of the French and British armies, and to the capital city of France. The initiative rested with him: he could choose both the point and the moment of attack; he could support it anywhere with superior numbers; neither the French nor ourselves could retreat without the risk of serious disaster. Ludendorff and Hindenburg had promised their countrymen the luxury of a knock-out blow. That blow has been delivered and has failed. The enemy has lost more ground than he gained in the opening days of his last offensive. He has lost in prisoners, wounded and killed, a larger number, in all probability, than we have any idea of. He has lost the initiative. But the greatest loss of all is the blow that has been inflicted upon the *moral* of his troops and the prestige of his country. Of course he still has very considerable reserves. His military position and his prestige are equally at stake, and he will make every endeavour to retrieve the position. It is too early to talk of victory, too early to imagine that the enemy is beaten; but it is true that the situation has changed. There is a break in the clouds, and the sun is riding high in the heavens.

This change in the situation has been due, in the main, apart from the uniform gallantry of the fighting forces of the Allies, to two factors: first, to the strategy of General Foch, and, secondly, to the magnificent response of America. In General Foch the Allies would appear to have found a Generalissimo—a few months ago we boggled at the name, but we now confidently and gratefully accept it—who combines those qualities of accurate intuition, quick decision, great moral courage, and the power of inspiring his troops with confidence, which have been characteristics of the great commanders in history.

In America we have found an ally of whom we are proud, and who has every reason to be proud of herself. For nearly three years, for reasons best known to themselves, which we do not presume to criticise, the Americans held aloof from a war in which the sympathies of the vast majority of their people were always on our side. Rather more than a year ago they came in. Then ensued a period in which little or nothing seemed to be done. Disappointment was expressed by their friends, gibes and jeers were indulged in by the enemy. But, with the events that began on the 21st of March, the American effort leapt at a bound to its maximum. The lid was taken off the cauldron which had been simmering for so long, and from it a flood of red-hot manhood, boiling over with virile energy and righteous indignation, was poured forth on to the battle-grounds of Europe. Such a spectacle has never before been seen in history. It came so suddenly. It was not the appearance of a regiment, of an army corps, of an army, but of a nation in arms. The effect was electric. The material value was enormous in changing the enemy's superiority, first, to a state of equality, and, secondly, as time passes, to one of numerical inferiority. The military and strategical value was great, in converting a rearguard action into an active counter-offensive. But the moral value was greatest of all in its effect upon the spirit both of the enemy and of the Allies. And this will be a cumulative effect, for, as the months pass by and hundreds of thousands of splendid men are landed on the shores of France, the Allies will be heartened and the enemy will be correspondingly depressed in the later stages of the War.

I invite you to consider how this great acceleration of American effort has been effected. First, let us pay our tribute to President Wilson for his foresight and courage, so much greater than our own, in the early introduction of compulsory military service in America, which enabled the men to be forthcoming. When we halted and wavered, he struck. Nor must we forget the steps which he took to seize German shipping in American harbours and to build up American shipping as well. All this is true, but it is also true that this great feat of transportation, which has changed the face of the War and given promise of ultimate victory, could never have been accomplished but for the British Navy and British shipping. We were told the other day that more than 1,000,000 American troops have been landed in France, the great majority of them in the last few months. Let me tell you that nearly 60 per cent. of these have been brought by British tonnage. In this month (July) alone we are carrying 200,000 American soldiers to France. In April we had 56 ships bringing American troops. In the month of July we have had 170. This great procession of ships, crossing thousands of miles of ocean in regular formation, presenting a large and visible target for attack, hunted and harried as they enter the danger zone by an invisible and desperate foe, but guarded by an ever-moving screen for the most part of British destroyers and British men-of-war, and weekly landing its complement of men in the ports of England

and of France, is one of the most impressive spectacles of the War. It reflects equal credit upon the British Navy, who have guarded the passage and held off the enemy; upon the Minister of Shipping, whose consummate organisation and efficient handling of tonnage have been mainly responsible for the supply of ships; and, lastly, upon the captains and men of the British Mercantile Marine. If ever a new edition is required of Captain Mahan's immortal work, a chapter may well be added on this convincing demonstration of what sea-power means.

But this is only one illustration of the contribution that has been made by Great Britain, unadvertised, for the most part unseen, and often quite unknown, to the Allied cause. I am tempted to say a few words on this subject. I pass over the fact that, alone of the Allies, we are fighting no fewer than seven campaigns, some of them at a distance of many thousands of miles from our shores—France and Flanders, Italy, Salonica, Palestine, Mesopotamia, Persia and East Africa. I pass over the more than 8,000,000 men whom we have raised in this country for all the purposes of war. I say nothing of the 3,000,000 British soldiers who are now serving abroad. Not one of these men is fighting on British soil. Each one of them is risking his life—thousands of them have already shed their life blood—for the defence and the emancipation of foreign peoples and foreign lands. Truly we may be said to have proved ourselves the knights-errant of civilisation. I do not wish to speak of that. I wish to speak rather of our contribution to the success of others. We are so deservedly loud in praise of the splendid efforts of our Allies that we are apt to forget our own virtues. There is much to be said for the saving grace of humility, but it is a doctrine that is capable of being pushed too far. I submit to you that we are entitled to a good conceit of ourselves. I cannot imagine a more interesting subject for an essay than a summary of the contributions that have been made in so many directions by Great Britain to the common cause. I have in my own mind a sketch of how such a statement might be framed. I would point out that this country is the feeder, the clothier, the carrier, the banker, the armourer, the Universal Provider of all our Allies.

Take the case of France alone. We cannot sufficiently express our admiration for the spirit and resolution with which the people of France have over and over again resisted and repelled the invasions of the enemy. We admire her veteran and indomitable Prime Minister, the skill of her commanders, the bravery of her troops, the patriotism and self-sacrifice of her citizens. We are proud to fight by their side and in their cause. But, without our aid, this superb effort could never have been made or sustained. Last year we carried to France 45 per cent. of her entire imports, and the same proportion to Italy. We carry to her shores over 50 per cent. of the coal by which her furnaces and forges, her railways and arsenals, are fed. We carry over 60 per cent. of the cereals by which her armies and her civil population are kept alive. We have at this moment 1,000,000 tons of shipping in the service of France, and half a million tons in the service of Italy. We carry to France an enormous amount of the railway material which she uses, the steel and iron—no fewer than 2,000,000 tons of the latter in the last year and a half—of machine-guns and trench mortars, and every variety of munitions of war, including no fewer than 120,000,000 rounds of small arms ammunition in the year 1917. This has nothing to do with the British army in France. We supply her with the blankets, the socks, the woollen clothes, the cotton and jute, with which her people are clothed. We are responsible for the entire supply of petrol and frozen meat which are required for her forces at Salonica.

And what we have done for her we have done, and are doing, for all the Allies. Since the beginning of the War we have carried 24,000,000 tons of stores for the Allies alone. The total value in the last year of the goods which we have supplied on special contract for the Allies has amounted to £17,000,000. To Italy, apart from our fighting army, we have sent thousands of guns and machine-guns, hundreds of thousands of rounds of ammunition, and an immense quantity of explosives. The bootmakers of Northampton and Kettering and Leicester have supplied the greater part of the footgear with which the Allied armies are shod. Since the beginning of the War they have turned out 60,000,000 pairs of boots. Similarly, the mills of Yorkshire—Huddersfield, Bradford, Leeds—and many other places, have furnished the clothing with which the Allied armies are clad. The Serbian soldier, who will shiver during the forthcoming winter in the highlands of Monastir, wears a fur coat and cap that come from Great Britain. The Roumanian soldier, before the collapse of his country, wore a British shirt. We have supplied 2,000,000 respirators to the Italian Army to enable them to breathe the air of victory within the forthcoming twelve months. To Russia, as my noble friend Lord Milner could tell you, we sent 700 guns and howitzers, 12,000,000 rounds of ammunition, and thousands of sets of artillery harness, the greater part of them, alas! engulfed in the appalling morass in which the destinies of that unhappy country have been plunged. The Chinese coolie who works behind the lines in France, the Kaffir boy from the Cape, the Portuguese and the Siamese soldier who is fighting with the Allies, wears a British-made dress or uniform. In this contribution great credit is due to our Dominions over the seas, to Australia, New Zealand and South Africa, who allowed us to purchase their entire wool clip for the purpose of the War. Nor, in the presence of the Air Minister, must I forget the Royal Air Force over which he presides, who have supplied a training staff, machines, engines and accessories to our Allies in every part of the world, including as many as 700 completed aeroplanes.

How have we been able to do this? The whole of this economic service depends upon our command of the seas. It has been secured by the predominance of the British Navy. Had we lost the command of the sea we could not have helped our Allies to fight; we could not even have kept our own population alive. The Navy has kept the seas open for the Mercantile Marine, and the Mercantile Marine has been the life-preserver of our Allies.

In this enumeration I had almost forgotten the financial assistance which we have been enabled to render. This "nation of shopkeepers" has kept open shop for the entire world. But we have also been the bankers who have placed them in funds. I recall that only a few days ago the Chancellor of the Exchequer stated in the House of Commons that since the beginning of the war we have advanced £1,370,000,000 to our Allies, and £206,000,000 to the Dominions. British credit has been the mainstay of the Alliance. Our advances have relieved them of the necessity of raising funds in their own countries. Our credit has enabled them to obtain supplies of raw material, of food, and the implements of war, from all the world. The financing of our Allies for the past four years has, in fact, been one of the great achievements of the War. Nor can it be said that we have done this for selfish reasons or for profit to ourselves. Had we not been manufacturing for our Allies we should have been manufacturing for export and for the upkeep of our own trade. To help others, we have temporarily dislocated our trade: some branches of it have been altogether ruined. We have had to reduce our own consumption and to ration our coal—and how serious that sacrifice has been the forthcoming winter will show. We have had to sell or pledge British securities and to incur severe losses in foreign countries.

I have spoken of the contribution that we have made in respect of shipping, of material, and of money. Do not let us forget the sacrifice of men. We are sometimes reproached for the number of men who are kept in this country. They are retained here not to defend our shores, but because they are carrying out invaluable and necessary service for our Allies. At the present time there are 260,000 men in this country engaged solely in industrial service for the Allies. Of the 375,000 men who are employed in digging coal, of the 1,000,000 men who are engaged in industrial work for the Admiralty, of the 1,500,000 men who are employed by my friend the Minister of Munitions on munition work, a large proportion are working not for us alone, but for the Allies as well. When we contemplate this accumulated effort, the most gigantic that this country has ever put forth, the wonder is that our military effort has been so great, and that, in addition to taking so large a share in the joint campaigns, we have been able to conduct three or four separate campaigns as well.

I submit that this great effort should be equally known to our own people and to our Allies. I doubt if, at present, it is at all adequately recognised by either. In four years it has built up the great fabric of military resistance which has enabled us to hold the enemy in check in Europe and to throw him back in defeat and disaster in so many other parts of the world. It finds us, after four years, weary, it is true, of war, because no one would wish to protract for an hour longer than is necessary so agonising a struggle for which so terrible a price has had to be paid. It finds us anxious for peace, provided it is the kind of peace to which we can honourably consent. But it also finds us with unabated resolution, with a fidelity to our friends and Allies which has never for a moment been shaken, and with a determination, which we share with them, to persevere without relenting until we attain the common goal. At the beginning of the fifth year of war we go forward with pride in our achievements, with gratitude to our own people and to our Dominions for the splendid response that they have made to our appeal, and with unaltered confidence in the justice and righteousness of our cause. Do I err if I say that there also enters into our hearts some spirit of exaltation that transcends the din of the workshops, the roar of the battlefield, and enables us to vanquish the worries and troubles of our everyday life? We feel that we are fighting for something bigger than the War itself, bigger, even, than the peace by which we hope it will be followed. A new world is in process of being built up out of the smoking and battered ruins of the old; and it will be a pride to those of us who are privileged to play a part in these great events that we have been among the architects and masons who are setting up this edifice. If that be so, it will be our consolation for all our efforts and losses and sacrifices: it will be to us a great and crowning and sufficient reward.

MASTER THE RIGHT HON. LORD JUSTICE DUKE next proposed "The Outer Dominions." He said: Mr. Junior, your Excellency, my Lords and Gentlemen. I am sure I may say with the approval of my colleagues here that if for five centuries and a half of recorded history we have observed the attitude of reserve to which Lord Curzon has alluded it has not been wholly due to that saving grace of humility with which he justly credited the legal profession. It is for other reasons that reticence has for five centuries and a half been observed here. There were not occasions like that of to-night to disturb our silence in the past, but the reticence of the past did not weaken the momentum of effort which the Inns of Court, and this Inn among them, were wont to bring to their share in the affairs of the country. It is five hundred years ago since Chief Justice Gascoigne assisted to conduct the affairs of Gray's Inn and of England. His name is a synonym for liberty and ordered independence. It is between three and four hundred years ago that the great Lord Burghley, as William Cecil, went forth from this House to build up the resources and powers of this country against foreign tyranny, and he succeeded under trials well-nigh as urgent as the trials of to-day, when our forefathers felt the perils of the Armada, as their children in our time encounter a foe as merciless. It is a good hundred years ago since Samuel Romilly, who was a Master of this Bench, built up that reputation for the humanity of our British justice or at any rate laid its foundation which is part of our inheritance. It was not for lack of achievement that our predecessors kept silence. There are incidents in the life of this Inn which it stirs the mind to remember. Francis Bacon was a Master here. William Shakespeare produced for the first time one of his comedies in this Hall. In the garden of Gray's Inn which remains to this day Walter Raleigh, after he had opened the way for civilisation in North America, walked while he discussed the affairs of the time with Francis Bacon. Bacon, or one of his biographers, tells us how he stayed chatting in the Walks with Raleigh while Robert Cecil was waiting for him in his chamber. These are little incidents which, while they may not distinguish us from other Inns, show, at any rate, that we have no reason for any shame. We have observed the Biblical precept that there is a time for silence, and we observe to-night the other Biblical precept, that there is a time to speak. We who have arrived at this night after four years of national effort and anguish can look back with satisfaction to the achievements, not only of England or of Britain, but of the British people, and the brotherhood of free men rooted throughout the world which makes up the British Empire. I have the honour to propose to you "The Outer Dominions." Some of us recall, and I do not think any man who witnessed it can ever forget, the scene in the House of Commons four years ago when Sir Edward Grey, with emotion which was visible, informed us that we were committed by every cause and obligation to which as Britons we had pledged ourselves in times of peace, to the most awful conflict the world had seen. We did not know the extent of the adventure. We knew there was an international conspiracy to set up brigandage in place of international law, to establish national blackmail instead of civil comity, and if not to hold individuals for ransom as the banditti of past days did, to hold states to ransom. Men who despised both divine and human law were prepared to make a pawn of a civilised State, and to hold its people to ransom. That was, I think, the greatest crisis in the history of the world. Our people faced the risk. The House of Commons that night cast its voice, in the name of Britain, and without dissent, to fight for humanity against organised international crime. We must have failed if the Dominions of the Empire had not stood by us. There would have been no four years of war. There might have been one year, but there would have been an epoch of disaster and destruction of everything which makes existence possible. The Dominions stood by the Motherland. To-day, as for so long now, we have their soldier sons on every pavement, as they come across to join the ranks or as they go back with their honourable wounds. I do not know that there is anything which one feels more than the opportunity of saying how proud one is to be their fellow-citizen. These tall, lithe fellows from all the Dominions of the Crown, and from every region of the Empire, have "come in." It is because of this the opportunity has been given of our assembling here not only with members of our own Government, but with representatives of our kinsmen in the United States and of our Allies, and the representatives of the Empire who sit day by day in the War Cabinet. Because of that opportunity to-night there is a time for speech. That there is a time for speech is proved by the marvellous address just delivered which is fresh in our minds. It is a fine speech because, as Lord Curzon says, we are at the beginning of a new era. The conspiracy against which we strive will find its doom, not, perhaps, this year, not, perhaps, next year, but it will find its inevitable doom. You cannot found in hell a human policy which shall reach up to heaven and endure. In this crisis of our fate it is a fortunate thing for the Empire that His Majesty's advisers have among them men like Sir Robert Borden, General Smuts and Mr. Hughes. There is a saying that if you want to go tiger-hunting you must choose your companions. The British race are out tiger-hunting and they have found noble comrades. Sir Robert Borden and General Smuts are here. Our colleague, Mr. Hughes, I am sorry to say, is ill. They are three statesmen of an Empire which, as an Empire, was supposed by some not to exist; an Empire as to which we can say with devout confidence to-night "Esto Perpetua." We are justified in that confidence by the past services of our fellow-citizens in every Dominion of the British Crown, by the fact that the citizens of the Dominions beyond the seas have sent to the Councils of our common King, statesmen such as Sir Robert Borden, General Smuts and Mr. Hughes. I have the honour to propose the toast of "The Outer Dominions," and I do it with the more intense pleasure because of the presence of the statesmen whose names it is my privilege to couple with the toast.

SIR ROBERT BORDEN (Prime Minister of Canada), rising to respond to the toast, said: Mr. Junior, your Excellency, my Lords and Gentlemen. I understand there are other engagements awaiting a number of those who sit around these tables this evening, and therefore it becomes me to make the briefest of replies to the toast which has been so eloquently proposed by my Lord Justice. I am very grateful for the opportunity to be here and to say a few words on behalf of the great Dominion I have the honour to represent. Standing here to-night within these ancient walls one cannot but be reminded of all the mighty events touching the Empire which have transpired. It was two and a quarter centuries after good Queen Bess associated herself with Gray's Inn that the mighty republic which adjoined our Dominion came into being. It was half a century afterwards before the self-governing Dominions of the Empire entered upon the principles of self-government which have developed to the greatest possible extent so that they are justly regarded as sister nations of the great British Continent. It is to me an inspiration to feel that comrades from that great sister republic are to-day fighting on the soil of France, and in Belgium, beside the men of this Empire, and especially by the side of the men of our Dominions. It has always been an aspiration to me since I entered public life some twenty-two years ago that Canada might in the years to come be a bond of unity between that great sister republic of the Empire Commonwealth and the British nation. And it is not the least of the issues which I think may come from this war that a truer understanding and a forgetfulness of differences in the past may come to that great nation and the Commonwealth to which we in Canada proudly own our allegiance. If that cannot come out of this War I do not know what can come, and if these two great nations can justify the public opinion which I am sure prevails in each by so acting with common purpose in the future for the preservation of the peace of the world, I do not doubt that the peace of the world will come and will be preserved by their effort. Lord Justice Duke has spoken of the great events of nearly four years ago when that grave announcement was made in the House of Commons by Sir Edward Grey. We in Canada had no more hesitation about our part in this War than you had here. I felt that I knew the spirit of the Canadian people sufficiently well to justify me on the first day of August, three days before War was declared, in sending on behalf of the Government and the people of Canada a message to the Government of the United Kingdom that if War should by any unhappy chance come, we in Canada would stand with you to the end. Not one of us realised at that time the tremendous character of the task that lay before us. You did not realise it here. The War has gone on for nearly four years. Sorrow, sacrifice, absolutely undreamt of, and untold of burdens beyond comprehension, have been endured by the Canadian people, and endured willingly and gladly for the cause which we are supporting. The spirit of our people was stern and determined when we first entered into this War four years ago. It is still firm and undaunted, and I venture to bring to you to-night from my own people beyond the Atlantic this message. They know and they realise more fully than ever before perhaps that the task before them is an exceedingly great one. The cost may entail even greater sacrifice than we can anticipate, but they will count all that we have endured and suffered as absolutely in vain unless we fight this War out to that conclusion which will justify the cause for which it was undertaken. I think that perhaps we in Canada and our brothers in the United States understand each other about as well as any two peoples in the civilised world. We were brought up under the same conditions, we were confronted with the same problems, we are united by the same ties, by ties of kinship, and a constantly increasing social and commercial intercourse. And if I might venture with very great respect to say a word on their behalf, I believe that the spirit of the United States is precisely that which I have just described to you. We are with you to the end. The end may be still a little distant. As to what that end will be none of us have any doubt, and if any man should have doubt, let him go to the troops at the Front, to the men who are holding the battle-line there, and he will come back with fresh inspiration, courage and confidence. And so God speed us all in the great work which lies before us.

GENERAL SMUTS said: Mr. Junior, my Lords and Gentlemen. I join with my friend Sir Robert Borden in thanking Lord Justice Duke for the very eloquent tribute he has paid to the Dominions. In all fairness to the Dominions, I have to admit that the praise has not been undeserved. I think that no praise could possibly be too high for these young Dominions which, far removed from the scenes of war, flung themselves from the first day with the enthusiasm of youth—with all their resources, into the great struggle, and have remained there since. But at the same time I wish to join with Lord Curzon in a tribute which I think is still more highly deserved and that is the tribute which is due to the people of this country. I think Lord Curzon is perfectly right when he says that not sufficient publicity has been given to that mighty effort. The British people are themselves, I won't say a shy people, but they are a reserved people and they prefer to praise others and not to refer to themselves or their own efforts, and the result has been that so far as public recognition is concerned their effort has to some extent gone by default. Speaking on behalf of the Dominions, we wish to say that words fail us in expressing our admiration for the mighty effort that has been made by this little island. Lord Curzon has gone into particulars as to those efforts. Let me sum it up in a couple of sentences as far as I am able to do so. When you started this War you were supreme on the seas with a Navy which throughout the whole struggle has remained the mainstay of our victory. You started first, you have continued first, and you will remain first, throughout this mighty struggle. On land you started as a nation of shopkeepers. During the past four years you have raised for War purposes, as Lord Curzon has said, 8,000,000 of people, and I believe I am correct in saying that to-day you, who started as a nation of shopkeepers, in this little island, have of all the Allies the greatest army in the field. During the War fighting has been transferred to a new element, and the air has become one of the most important theatres of the War. You started at a very low level in this phase when War broke out, but the ceaseless effort of your people have succeeded in creating not only a formidable organisation of air fighting, but I believe I may say without any exaggeration the most formidable fighting Air Force on the Allied side. When I add to this that you are the only nation engaged in the War who have actually increased their capacity for food-production during the War, I think I have summed up the main features of the great and mighty effort that has been made by the people of this country. It has been made silently, with calmness, with dignity, and without any publicity, but with that settled resolution and determination which have characterised the nation in all the crises where it knew it was up against fate, and was determined to see the business through. All classes of the country, men, women and children, from the highest to the lowest, have proved faithful and true in the tremendous struggle through which they have gone. They have proved themselves true to themselves, to their country, and to those high ideals which have made this country the home and the treasury of free institutions for a large part of the world. These free institutions have spread throughout the world in what we know as the British Empire—in North America, South Africa and the Pacific, all bound together with this little island in one great institution of Freedom, and it has been your great effort in the past to make this great free Commonwealth to which we belong a more magnificent institution than has ever before been possible on the face of the earth, greater than that Roman Empire, greater than any Empire that has ever existed. It is great, not only in population, in territory, in material resources, but it is great because of the ideals upon which it is founded—the ideals of liberty and self-government and honour and freedom on which it is founded, and which have underlaid all its efforts in the past. It is because this nation and the nations which have sprung from it believed in human liberty, and trusted human nature and its capacity to work out its own regeneration; it is because of that that you have become in this great struggle, which is largely a moral struggle, the mainstay of the Allied cause. We have known of liberty and freedom as an ideal in the past, but it has been the achievement of this country, this small island, and of the other nations which it has founded, to bring that ideal down from the clouds, to make that ideal a reality, to make that human liberty an institution, a great organised institution in which so large a portion of the human race to-day is found. It is our dearest wish, and our determination, that that organised institution of freedom and liberty shall continue to exist after this War. That institution is being tested to-day, and tested to the uttermost, and it is our determination that we shall win through—that we shall win not only material victory, and a military victory, but that we shall also win a moral victory. And then when we are through this great struggle, those ideas on which our system is founded will continue to be stronger and better, and will from us proceed forward to influence the other nations of the world. It is not necessary for me, I hope, to say much more. It is difficult to-day to forecast events. We are to-day on the upgrade. The curve is going up, but no wise man will say what the immediate future will produce. War is a curve which goes up and down; our curve may to-morrow go down again, but we are determined whatever our curve may be, to put all our strength into the struggle to obtain a victory which will safeguard the great free institution of the British Empire as it exists to-day. We are determined to see that military force shall fail and to bring it home to the German people, and the rulers of Germany, that in this great contest which they have themselves called forth, with force on one side and the freedom of nations on the other, they must fail, and when they have failed, then, indeed, the British Empire with all its branches will have justified itself, and its example set to the world will be followed by other nations.

THE TREASURER said without adding to the toast list, he was going to ask their good friends the Italian Ambassador, and Mr. Franklin Roosevelt, as representing the great American nation, to say a few words.

THE ITALIAN AMBASSADOR in responding said the fact that he had been asked to speak reminded him of the gentleman who arrived at a dinner with the object of having a specially pleasant evening and enjoying the speeches, but who was suddenly called upon to speak himself. That was exactly his position, and it would be presumption on his part to attempt to address them in English after so many excellent speeches. Reference has been made (he said) to the part which my countrymen have contributed to this Great War, and to the great cause which we all have at heart, and are doing our utmost to defend and to further to a successful issue. I was pleased to hear what the noble Lord Curzon said about the contribution which this country has made to the cause of the Allies during the War. I can assure you the Allies feel most grateful for that assistance, and that we shall never forget it. We have done our best to deserve it and for the cause for which we are all fighting. One of our speakers has referred to the Roman Empire. It is absolutely true, as has been said, that it is because the people of the British Empire realise that it stands for freedom and justice, that they are fighting for the common cause. It is the same with us. We are with you because we realise, as one of the oldest friends of Great Britain, that you are fighting in the cause of justice and freedom. As to America, I may tell Mr. Roosevelt that my people from the bottom of their hearts have been moved by the extraordinary exertions which his great nation have made in the cause of the Allies, and to carry out a policy which, in the words of their President, will make the world safe for democracy.

MR. FRANKLIN ROOSEVELT said: Not only was I given to understand that I should not be called upon to speak, but since my connection with the Naval Service I have fallen somewhat into the same feeling that the First Lord has expressed to me—that we have become simple sailor-men and no longer speakers. But may I very simply, in a very few words, tell you how deeply glad I am to have this opportunity of coming to express the hope that many other members of our Government will come to England, and to France, and to Italy, because it is only in that way that we can obtain any adequate idea of the magnitude of the task which lies before us, and of the way in which we can best help our Allies to the final end. I must say that in the short week I have been here there has been brought home to me, through my very close association with the First Lord on a trip of inspection to Ireland, the necessity for more of this intimate personal relationship. It is quite impossible, as Sir Robert Borden knows, to sit at home 3000 miles or more away and to obtain that close man-to-man, shoulder-to-shoulder touch, which to-day characterises the work of the Allies in conducting the War. I may say, too, that I hope Sir Robert Borden will continue to speak for the Republic to the South of Canada. May I say to one who comes from the same stock that I do, a fellow Netherlander of many generations ago, that to-day the people of your blood in South Africa and the people of my blood of New Amsterdam, men in New York, that we are proud to fight with you. What I have seen in this short week emphasises more than all the documents and the telegrams and the cablegrams passing between my friends in the Admiralty and my own Navy Department during the past fifteen months that our Naval Forces are working together in a way which I think I can modestly describe as satisfactory. We are proud to have the opportunity to serve side by side with that great British Navy from which we spring, because the traditions of our Service are the traditions of the British Service, and I hope and know that at home the people of the United States will realise more clearly as the days and the weeks pass, that this feat of bringing over an army, now progressing at the rate of 300,000 a month, is due, as Lord Curzon has said, in the proportion of 60 per cent., to British transports. In providing ships we are, to be sure, increasing our efforts and are putting our shoulders to the wheel. We are with you—about ninety-nine and nine-tenths of 110,000,000 of our people are with you—in the declaration that we are going to see this thing through with you.

THE TREASURER in proposing the toast of the Bench said: The remaining toast of the evening is by no means the least important because it comes so late. It is the toast of "The Bench." The toast is naturally replied to in this Hall in the present circumstances by the Lord Chancellor. The Lord Chancellor has the respect of the whole profession. He led me many, many times, but I cannot even at a moment like this allow him to forget that I once led him. I even did him greater service in my youth because I dedicated to him a book which I had written! The Lord Chancellor preserves to us the ideas and highest traditions as they come down through many generations of Lord Chancellors who have been nestors alike of our political and legal life. He presides in the Highest Court, which is the Court alike of these islands and in the Judicial Committee of the Privy Council of the Empire. Our old friend Lord Halsbury would have been asked to reply to this toast if he had been able to attend. He wrote me in his own handwriting a long letter dealing with many subjects of the day. If he had been able to attend to-night he would have done so, and my Lord Chancellor will forgive me for saying what I have said in praise of the grand old man. In Mr. Justice Darling we have here one whose judicial career we have watched for so many years, and who has filled worthily the position of the Lord Chief Justice during his absence. We have also here to-night the President of the Probate Admiralty and Divorce Court. As Law Officer of the Crown it has been my duty to present cases before him in the Prize Court, and I may say with very great respect that his contributions to International Law will, in my humble judgment, last as long as the contributions of the great Lord Stowell. He has played a great part in this War, and I believe his name will always be honoured at these gatherings. I now give you the toast of "The Bench," coupled with the honoured name of the Lord High Chancellor.

THE LORD CHANCELLOR said: I never enjoyed a higher distinction than that of taking the place of our dear and honoured friend Lord Halsbury. His absence we all lament. I feel proud that it devolves on me to say what he would have said so much better. We have had a most inspiriting evening. We have breathed an ampler ether and now it falls to me to return thanks for the Bench of the country. I think I may say that no one can appreciate what England is, what the British Empire is, unless he has been present at a gathering of this kind. We don't know England unless we know what the British Empire is, and the gathering this evening has shown the British Empire gathered in this Hall, which has witnessed so many historic scenes. What I would venture to say is that never since the spacious times of the great Elizabeth has there been witnessed a more inspiriting and more inspiring gathering than that at which it has been our privilege to be present to-night. I think that what you (the Treasurer) have said is perfectly true—that the Bench of this country will do its duty in the future as it has done in the past. The independence of the English Bench has always been one of the great features of that ordered liberty which this country has always enjoyed. I am perfectly certain that that independence will continue to distinguish that great body whom I this evening have the honour to represent.

In proposing the health of "The Treasurer, Sir Frederick Smith," the Lord Chancellor said: We are all grateful to you (the Treasurer) for what you have said this evening. What you have said has rung out as a triumph note, as a signal for the Empire in these days of stress and strain—that the Empire will be true to itself and true to the great traditions which we have inherited, and of which we are rightly reminded when we meet in an old historic Hall like this. You have voiced the sentiments which animate every one of us in this Hall. What you have said should inspirit us with all enthusiasm to drink your health and to wish you all prosperity, and many a long year of success in that career which lies before you.

THE TREASURER, in reply, said: It is, my Lord Chancellor, a source of great satisfaction to me that the toast which you have proposed should have been so generously accepted. It would be idle of me to pretend that in these anxious years, during which I have discharged the responsible duties of principal Law Officer of the Crown, I have not had to face constant difficulties and anxieties, amounting almost to crises, in every department over which I have presided. That I have so far escaped without open disaster is due largely to those around me on whom I have relied for help continuously. I hope I have been able to do my duty not entirely without success. I shall always look back to the position which I occupy as Treasurer of this great foundation as one of the proudest of my life—that I should have been invited to become the Treasurer of this ancient House. The sincere manifestation to-night is one of which I shall always cherish the recollection amid these terrible years of War—that I should have been honoured to preside at your gathering.

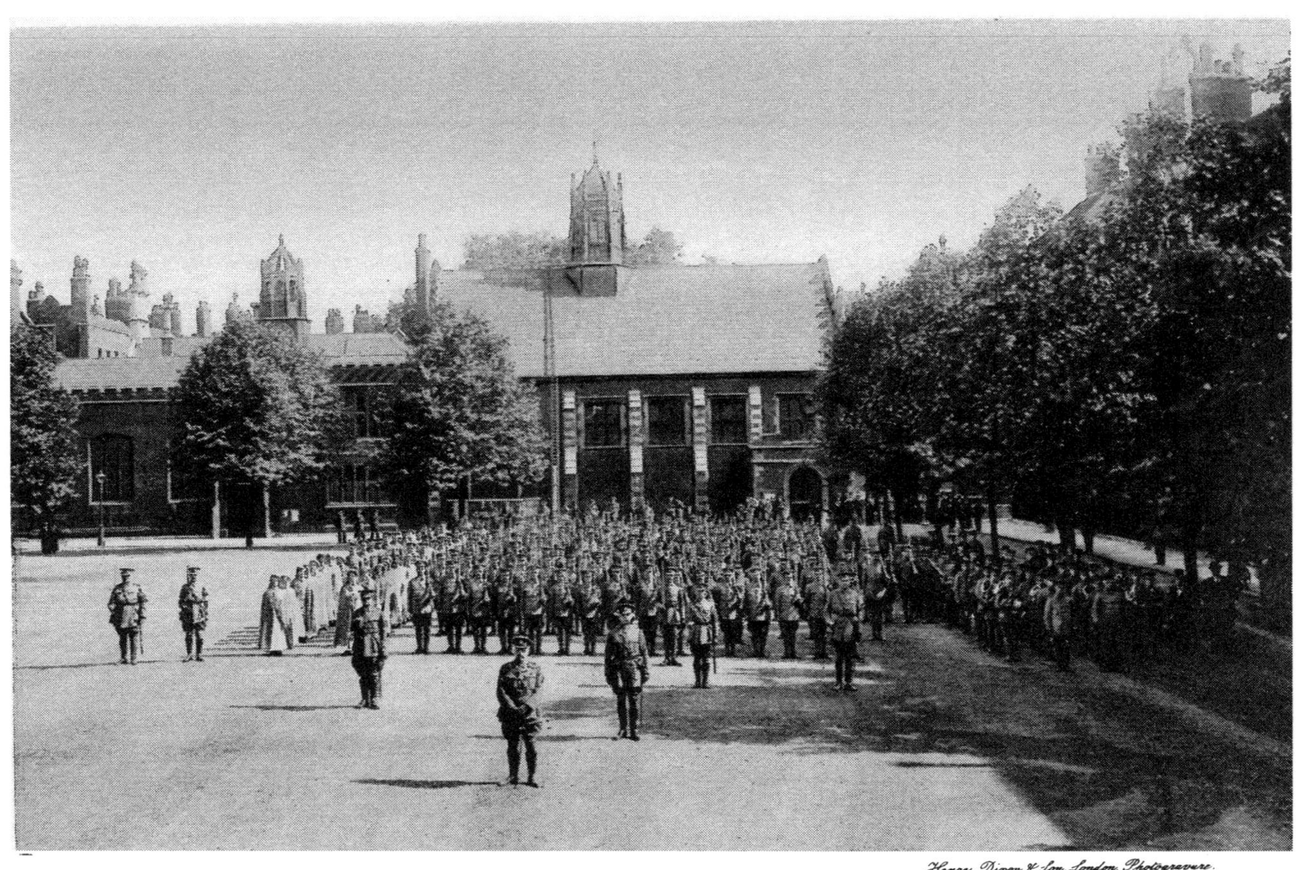

Henry Dixon & Son. London. Photogravure.

Gray's Inn Square — The Holborn Volunteer Battalion.

DECEMBER 20th, 1918.

The Hon. John W. Davis, the Ambassador of the United States of America in succession to Mr. Page, landed in this country on the 16th of December.

A distinguished jurist and Solicitor-General of the United States since 1913, Mr. Davis was intimately associated with the Treasurer of Gray's Inn on the occasion of his tour through the States in the winter of 1917–18, and it was desired to welcome him at Gray's Inn upon his arrival.

At short notice a luncheon in Hall was arranged for the 20th of December, which the Ambassador attended as the principal guest. There was no report in the Press, but a note of the proceedings was taken which is printed in the following pages.

SPEECHES

AT A LUNCHEON TO THE HON. JOHN W. DAVIS, AMBASSADOR OF THE UNITED STATES OF AMERICA, GIVEN IN GRAY'S INN HALL ON THE AFTERNOON OF THE 20th OF DECEMBER, 1918.

The Treasurer (the Right Hon. Sir Frederick Smith, Bart., K.C., M.P., Attorney-General) presided, supported by most of the Masters of the Bench. There was also a large attendance of Members of the Society in Hall.

The following guests were present: The Lord Chancellor (Lord Finlay); Lord Halsbury; the Lord Chief Justice (The Earl of Reading); Lord Haldane; Lord Mersey; Lord Buckmaster; Lord Cave; the Master of the Rolls (Lord Sterndale); Mr. Justice Eve; the Solicitor-General (Sir Gordon Hewart, K.C., M.P.); Sir John Simon, K.C.; and Mr. Leslie Scott, K.C. After the toast of "The King"—

THE TREASURER said: We have to-day the privilege of entertaining a guest of very great distinction—a guest who should be, and will be, welcomed with great cordiality in any assembly of English lawyers. He held high office as Solicitor-General in the United States of America with a degree of legal accomplishment which has seldom been equalled in the history of the law officers of the United States, and it is indeed fortunate for us in this country that at this moment—still grave, though less critical than it was—at this moment, the most critical that we have been confronted with in the history of the world, it is indeed fortunate that the representative of the United States in this country should be a gentleman of the ability, and of the attachment to this country which I know well, and all his friends know well, the new Ambassador possesses. Mr. Junior, this is not the occasion for formal speechmaking, nor do I propose to attempt to make a speech, but I say, as the Treasurer of this Inn, that I shall be expressing the feeling of all the members of this Inn when I assure this distinguished representative of that great, virile and unselfish Republic, whose intervention has won this War, and without whose intervention we could not to-day be celebrating our victory—if I tell him on an occasion when he meets the barristers and students of this Inn, that he meets some of the most distinguished ornaments of the Bench in this country gathered here to offer him welcome. I say this to him—that we receive him in this country with a degree of warmth and friendship which it is not possible at this moment exactly to measure and appraise, but every week and month he spends here will teach him how great that cordiality is and how unanimous is the determination among the people of this country to see to it that no single cause of difference shall mar the harmony which must exist in the interests of civilisation and the world between these two great Anglo-Saxon communities. We are not so oblivious to what is happening to-day, and not so oblivious to what has happened in the past, as not to be well aware that there are many causes which could be made the occasion of differences between the two countries. We are not unaware there are some people in both countries who are prepared to make the most of such causes of friction which exist, but of this we are certain—that the overwhelming majority of the citizens of your country, and the overwhelming majority of the citizens of our country, are determined that this War, which has established so many new precedents, has established for once and for all time a new era in the relations between the United States of America and Great Britain. Sir, you will make many friends in this country. Wherever you go you will make friends, but I am glad indeed to think, and I am proud as Treasurer of this Inn to recall, that there will be entered upon the records of the War history of this Inn, that we had the privilege first of all to welcome you in this country, and I hope, sir, that in the course of your stay here it will not be the last occasion that we shall welcome you. In asking you, gentlemen, to charge your glasses to the health of the new American Ambassador, I ask you to do honour to an illustrious lawyer, to one who I am sure will be a great diplomatist, and of whom I confidently and dogmatically say that no American who has come to this country in recent years will prove himself to be more sympathetic to this Island and to this Empire.

THE AMBASSADOR, in reply, said: Mr. Treasurer, my Lords and Gentlemen. Sir Frederick will tell you that when I accepted, as I did with eagerness, the invitation to attend this luncheon it was with the distinct understanding that I should not be called upon to speak. For this I advanced the very good reason that I had stated elsewhere that I would under no circumstance accept any invitation to make any speech until the New Year. But Sir Frederick's persuasions are hard indeed to resist, and even though I had been charged in advance with the duty of making a speech I could not have foregone this invitation, nor could I at this moment forgive myself, if I remained silent after the generous welcome you have extended to me and the more than kind language which your distinguished Treasurer has used in reference to myself. I am a newcomer among you. I reached the shores of England less than one week ago, but I have felt during every moment that I have been here that, after all, I was in truth at home. And in this presence I feel something even more than that. I feel that I am at home in my own house. If there is one spot in your country, or mine, which more than any other holds our common history, which more than any other is the focus of that community of sentiment and ideal, which, please God, will always bind our peoples, it is these Inns of Court where our common liberties were forged and fashioned by those members of our profession who have gone before. How could I feel otherwise than at home when I see on your walls such portraits as that of Lord Coke—the founder of our Common Law; or that of Francis Bacon, equally revered by English and American lawyers. May I venture a word of personal reminiscence. During my incumbency of the office of Solicitor-General it became my pleasing duty in the absence of my chief to transmit to a personal friend his commission as a judge upon our Federal Bench. I accompanied it with a letter expressing my gratification that fortune permitted me in signing his commission to associate my name with his in his new office. And I added: "I believe you to be highly competent for this responsible position, but qualified you will not be until you can assure me that you have read, marked and inwardly digested as the best pabulum for a judge, new or old, Francis Bacon's *Essay on Judicature.*"

It is in such circumstances that I find myself to-day responding to the cordial words of your Treasurer. I shall not attempt to make a speech, but I renew my expression of deep gratification at the cordiality of your welcome and I associate myself with all the vigour of my soul with what your Treasurer has said concerning the unity of sentiment, ideals and purpose between your great people and ours in this new world that opens before us. Let it never be thought the American people do not realise the greatness of the struggle you have made or the sacrifices you have endured. The boundless courage you showed against our common foe was such that it will ever be in our minds. We are proud indeed that we are admitted to share with you in the final victory. Let us hope that in the years to come no thought, no word, no act may disturb that solidarity which should bless us, and in blessing us should bless the world.

F

MAY 9th, 1919.

On the 10*th of January*, 1919, *the Attorney-General* (*The Right Hon. Sir Frederick Smith, Bart., K.C., M.P.*) *was appointed Lord High Chancellor of Great Britain in the Second Administration of Mr. Lloyd George, formed after the General Election of December*, 1918, *and upon his elevation to the Peerage, which immediately followed, he took the title of Lord Birkenhead of Birkenhead in the co. of Chester. In June*, 1921, *he was raised to the dignity of a Viscount of the United Kingdom.*

The career of Lord Birkenhead is unique in the romantic annals of the English Bar.

Frederick Edwin Smith was born at Birkenhead on the 12*th of July*, 1872. *In his eighteenth year he matriculated at Wadham College, Oxford, having previously been elected a classical scholar. He became President of the Union; obtained a first class in Jurisprudence; won the Vinerian Law Scholarship, and was made a Fellow of Merton College.*

Mr. F. E. Smith was admitted a Student at Gray's Inn on the 20*th of November*, 1894, *and was called to the Bar at Gray's Inn on the* 14*th of June*, 1899, *being bracketed second in the first Honours class. He joined the Northern Circuit, and in* 1906 *was elected Member of Parliament for the Walton Division of Liverpool. He was appointed one of His Majesty's Counsel in* 1908 (*less than nine years after call, which is, under modern conditions at least, a record*), *and immediately after was elected a Master of the Bench of Gray's Inn.*

Mr. F. E. Smith, K.C., M.P., was sworn of the Privy Council in 1911. *He served in France with the rank of Major in the Expeditionary Force from September* 1914 *to May* 1915, *and was mentioned in despatches in April. In May he was appointed Solicitor-General in Mr. Asquith's Coalition Government. Upon this occasion he received the honour of knighthood. He was promoted Attorney-General later in the same year and became a member of the Cabinet.*

The Right Hon. Sir Frederick Smith, K.C., M.P., was elected Treasurer of Gray's Inn for the year 1917, *and was re-elected Treasurer for the year* 1918. *He was created a Baronet in* 1918, *and again re-elected Treasurer of Gray's Inn for the year* 1919.

It was while he was filling his third term as Treasurer that he was raised to the great office of Lord High Chancellor, and the Bench, with the universal approval of Hall, resolved to celebrate the event by a House Dinner at which the Treasurer (*the Lord Chancellor*) *was the sole guest.*

The Dinner was held on the evening of the 9*th of May*, 1919.

Henry Dixon & Son, London. Photogravure.

The Right Hon. Lord Birkenhead, Treasurer of Gray's Inn. 1917–1919.

HOUSE DINNER

IN HALL TO THE TREASURER OF GRAY'S INN (THE LORD HIGH CHANCELLOR OF GREAT BRITAIN) UPON HIS ELEVATION TO THE WOOLSACK, ON THE EVENING OF THE 9th OF MAY, 1919.

The Senior Bencher (Master Judge Mulligan, K.C.) presided as Acting Treasurer, having upon his right the guest of the evening, the Treasurer of Gray's Inn, the Lord Chancellor.

The other Masters of the Bench present were: Mr. Henry Goudy, D.C.L.; Mr. M. W. Mattinson, K.C.; Sir Lewis Coward, K.C.; Mr. C. A. Russell, K.C.; The Hon. Mr. Justice Lush; Mr. Thomas Terrell, K.C.; Mr. W. T. Barnard, K.C.; The Right Hon. Lord Justice Duke; The Lord Chancellor of Ireland (The Right Hon. Sir James Campbell, Bart); Mr. Herbert F. Manisty, K.C.; Mr. Edward Clayton, K.C.; Mr. W. J. R. Pochin; Mr. Arthur E. Gill; Mr. E. F. Vesey Knox, K.C.; The Right Hon. Lord Justice Atkin; The Right Hon. Sir William Byrne, K.C.V.O., C.B.; Mr. Montagu Sharpe, D.L.; Mr. George Rhodes, K.C.; Mr. Charles Herbert-Smith; His Honour Judge Ivor Bowen, K.C.; Mr. W. Clarke Hall; Mr. R. E. Dummett; Sir Hamar Greenwood, Bart., K.C., M.P.; The Right Hon. A. W. Samuels, K.C., M.P. (Attorney-General of Ireland).

Mr. A. H. Lush was Senior in Hall, and the Hall to its utmost capacity was crowded with barristers and students, all members of the House. The members desiring to attend being much beyond the available room, many seats were assigned by ballot.

During the speeches, Lady Birkenhead and some of the Benchers' ladies had places in the Minstrel Loft.

After dinner the Acting Treasurer proposed the toasts, "The King," "The Queen, Queen Alexandra, the Prince of Wales and the other Members of the Royal Family."

The Acting Treasurer then gave the toast, "To the Memory of the Members of this Society who have fallen in the War." He said: Mr. Senior. In the very regrettable absence through illness of the Senior Bencher, Master Rose, it devolves upon me to propose the next toast, which is to the memory of the members of this Society who have fallen in the Great War. I will give their names—we should all have been thankful if they were less numerous—and will afterwards record such meagre particulars as have been ascertained. The names in alphabetical order are (he then read the names of the fallen, and proceeded):

I should like now, if I could, to say something of the part taken by each of those gallant members in the great conflict. But it is not possible. For their noble deeds in most cases are not known to us here, though they are doubtless accounted unto them elsewhere in a record invisible to the eye of man. It is little more than chance which, with the help of our Under-Treasurer, enables me to give the following details concerning a few of them—where they fought, and how they fell in the service of our country and our king.

Lieutenant Arnold H. Ball, who was killed on the 9th of April, 1918, aged twenty-nine, was the third son of the late W. E. Ball, Barrister-at-Law. He was educated at the City of London School, and was called to the Bar at Gray's Inn in 1910. He received his commission in the Territorial Force on the 30th of December, 1915, and went to the Front on the 30th of September, 1916. He remained on front-line duty, except for three periods of leave, until he was killed. You will remember, Mr. Senior, that his father in his later days worthily occupied the position of Senior Barrister in this Hall.

There are few members of this House killed in the War whose names were better known in Gray's Inn five years ago than George Thomas Ewen. Few members of his standing have taken a larger part in the life of the Inn. He served at one time or another as a member of all those Committees on which Junior Barristers and Students are represented. He made his own career, beginning at the very bottom of the ladder. When war broke out he had already entered the Chambers of a Chancery Barrister, who said of him that he had seldom met a man of quicker intelligence, saner judgment and greater power of application. He had to fight hard against the traditions of the army in the earlier stages of the War. There was an impression then that men over thirty were not suitable for commissions. Ewen overcame that barrier, as he had overcome others, and from junior subaltern he became brigade machine-gun officer in a very short space of time. He was a skilful mountaineer—a well-known member of the Alpine Club—he had made the traverse of the Matterhorn without a guide. His powers of endurance enabled him to withstand the almost superhuman trials of the first Mesopotamian campaign. He was mortally wounded there, and the last that is known of him is that he sent back his servant just before the trenches were overrun, saying to him, "I shall do very well." He did.

Captain H. M. Finegan was the most brilliant undergraduate of his time at Liverpool University. He was a Scholar, and took first-class honours in History. He also took honours in the LL.B. Examination. He was a fine athlete and a brilliant debater, and during 1913 and 1914 was President of the College of Undergraduates of the University. He was a prominent member of the Irish Society.

Sergeant-Major Frederic Hillersdon Keeling should be mentioned. Keeling's biography, as some of you know, has already been written. He was in some ways the most remarkable member of the Inn who has fallen in the War. He left Winchester as Head Boy with a Major Scholarship at Trinity College, Cambridge. He became a Fabian, and one of the most advanced members of that school. It was not of that material, as a rule, that the volunteers of August, 1914, were made. Keeling turned at once from vehement criticism of the existing social order and became a private in the army on the 6th of August. He rose to be company-sergeant-major and—according to his commanding officer—one of the best he ever had. He afterwards became sergeant-major of a bombing company, and he died leading his men in a bombing attack on a German trench. Three times he refused a commission. One of his biographers says: "When Keeling died the British Commonwealth (as he preferred to call it) lost one of its worthiest citizens. Though in the old days he was a State Socialist, yet his complex personality cherished liberty as its chief possession. No man had a stronger passion for liberty than he. Human liberty—that was the real motive behind all his work, and eventually he died for it."

Maung Maung was a Burman, and his is the only Eastern name in the list. His career was weird. Men of his race and colour were not admitted to the army in this country, but Maung would be in the fight, and by reason of his importunity he managed to become enrolled in the ranks of the London Irish. Being invalided out of the army he went back to Burma on recruiting work, and was drowned in the Irrawaddy while so employed.

Second-Lieutenant Leslie William Whitworth Quin received the Military Cross for conspicuous gallantry in action. He led a raiding party with great courage and skill, maintaining his position for an hour and a half. He set a splendid example to his men.

Cosmo George Romilly was called to the Bar in 1913. He was a member of the great family of English Jurists, of whom two have been Benchers and Treasurers of this Society—Sir Samuel Romilly and Lord Romilly. Another member, the Hon. Arthur Romilly, was called with me. He was of great promise, and if he had lived would have worthily handed down the lamp of liberty lighted by Sir Samuel.

Major Tremearne was author of the *Ban of the Bori* and several other interesting works on African folk-tales, superstitions and kindred subjects. If he had been spared he would doubtless have helped to trace back to their true springs the streams of Western civilisation.

Lieutenant Elias Tremlett had a very remarkable record. He was holder of the Inns of Court Studentship, Trinity, 1914; Arden Scholar, Gray's Inn, 1913; Holt Scholar, Gray's Inn, 1912; LL.B. and University Scholar, London University. Like others of great promise his career was prematurely ended.

The name of Lieut.-Commander Dawbarn Young is recorded in the epic which tells the story of the attack on the Mole at Zeebrugge on St. George's Day, 1918. He had volunteered to take a motor launch in advance of the block-ships, and to light their passage into the harbour by means of flares. On approaching the entrance his boat, M.L. 110, was struck by three shells. He was wounded in three places, but in spite of his injuries he remained at his post and continued to give his orders until he collapsed. He died before reaching Dover. Young spent the night in Gray's Inn before setting out on his great undertaking.

Mr. Senior, our knowledge of these young men is sparse and fragmentary. This much we do know—they had courage—the chiefest of the virtues. They were men indeed. In a war unequalled for its magnitude, and for the ferocious German efforts to undo Liberty for all time, our young members went forth, fought a good fight, and gave their lives for Freedom, for us, and for the ages that are to come. Their very mention, Mr. Senior, may recall to some of us a simile used by a great Athenian statesman. In speaking of the young men of Athens who had fallen in the Peloponnesian War, Pericles said: "They have perished from the city like the spring from the year." We may well say: These young members have perished from our House like the spring from the year. They will have a place in our memory until we meet again, after the great change which must come to us all. Mr. Senior, in silence, in silent veneration, let us drink to the memory of the members of this Society who have fallen in the War.

The toast "To the memory of the members of the Society who have fallen in the War" was then drunk in silence, all present standing.

After the toast of "Domus" had been honoured—

MASTER MATTINSON, K.C., in proposing the toast of the evening, "The Lord High Chancellor," said:—Mr. Senior, looking round this crowded Hall to-night I can with truth say that this is far and away the most remarkable and representative gathering of the Society of Gray's Inn during the forty-five years I have been a member of this House. It is a night to be remembered; one which will be historic in the annals of Gray's Inn.

I regard it as a high honour that to-night I am privileged as the mouthpiece of the Society to express on its behalf the feelings of pride and affection with which this ancient House greets its most distinguished son upon his attaining the great position in the State which his character and abilities have won. I am very sensible that there are men at this table better qualified than myself to give adequate expression to the sentiments which we all entertain towards the Lord Chancellor, but as a true lover of this old Inn I make this claim, that no one has or can have a more vivid appreciation than I of the splendid chapter which his brilliant career has added to the glorious roll of Gray's Inn.

Mr. Senior, in this Hall we are the heirs of a great tradition. That tradition is not dimmed in our day. To-night it shines with renewed lustre. We have just drunk in solemn silence to the memory of the gallant dead of Gray's Inn, but there is another thought of the past that rises in our minds to-night. Assembled in this venerable Hall, teeming with a thousand great memories, upon an occasion when we have met to congratulate one of our number who has won for himself an assured position in the history of his country as lawyer, statesman and orator, we should be unworthy of the great past if we did not for just one moment recall the mighty dead of Gray's Inn, men mighty in intellect, mighty in service to the State and to humanity, who in their day were of the fellowship of this House, who were proud to be of that fellowship, and whose name and fame are the undying tradition of Gray's Inn. Gascoigne, Cromwell, Burghley, Walsingham, Philip Sidney, Salisbury, Francis Bacon, Holt, Romilly—imperishable names while the story of England is told—and now to that great company of the immortals this generation adds the name of Birkenhead.

Mr. Senior, I, like many others of this House, am of the Northern Circuit. The Northern Circuit has given many Lord Chancellors to England, of whom our guest is the last. Perhaps in this Hall we may claim that Gray's Inn has given the Chancellor to the Northern Circuit but, at any rate, this is true of the Northern Circuit, that it at once took him whole-heartedly to its bosom. Liverpool gave him his first foothold in the profession, and an early entrance into public life. It is a remarkable circumstance that in 1589 Francis Bacon, then a young man of twenty-seven, was elected Member of Parliament for Liverpool, and after a long interval, in 1906, Frederick Edwin Smith, also a young man, was elected as a successor of Bacon in the representation of Liverpool. The successor of Bacon in the representation of Liverpool has been his successor at this Bench, his successor in that Chair, and his successor on the Woolsack. And this Society has pledged itself to the pious duty of providing that the visible portraiture of those two distinguished men, both of whom have illustrated the annals of this House, shall go down to remotest posterity side by side on that wall of this Hall.

One of the last Chancellors the Northern Circuit gave the profession was Henry Brougham. I am not going to attempt any comparison between those two Chancellors from the Northern Circuit, except to say that on one point I know our Chancellor from the Northern Circuit, as I hope I may call him, is wholly free from a weakness which was attributed to the great Brougham. It would, however, be no disparagement of our guest if I did contrast the two men, as in wide range of attainments and interests and versatility of genius, Brougham was probably the greatest man who held the office of Chancellor in the long interval from Bacon. It was said of him that he was a universal genius who would have known everything if he had known a little law. I say nothing about that. Its author was another Lord Chancellor, and it may be that this saying was only a further illustration of that remarkable appreciation of one another's defects which Bowen attributed to his judicial brethren. All that, however, is by the way. The criticism upon Brougham I have in my mind was one which Lord Campbell made in the *Life of Brougham*, which he contributed to his amiable series of Lives of the Chancellors—and here, Lord Chancellor, I would say that not the least of the many felicities of your career is this, that coming to the Woolsack in the twentieth century, and not in the eighteenth or nineteenth century, you have avoided the delicate biographical attentions of Lord Campbell, and so, as it was once put, have escaped one of the terrors of death. But poor Brougham was less fortunate, because Campbell proceeded to write his Life before he died;

and in that Life I fear it was with some malicious glee that he described Brougham—who was descended from a healthy Westmorland yeoman stock—as a man obsessed with the delusion that he was a person of the bluest blood, a patrician of the first water, whose ancestors came over, not with the Conqueror, but were possessed of their ancient estates in these islands when the Antonines ruled in Rome. It is very likely that Campbell put it on with a thick brush, but be that as it may, I know this of our Chancellor from the Northern Circuit, that there is no nonsense of that kind about him. It is his proud boast, that starting life without any adventitious aids from birth or fortune or patronage, he has won his own way and carved out his own fortune by the powers of his own mind and will.

There is a note of sincerity in our guest which appeals to this House. There is something else about him which equally appeals to this House. It was Lord Westbury who said that the greatest of all a man's attachments was to his Inn of Court. Now that was a sentiment which had too much feeling in it to seem altogether appropriate in the mouth of a man of Westbury's cynical mood, and it has been doubted whether he really meant what he said, but if our guest had said that, there is not one of us acquainted with him in this House who would have the least doubt of the perfect and entire sincerity of the utterance. I know that the Chancellor has a great affection for this House. I know its story appeals to his imagination, and I believe that not the least of his happiness in his hour of triumph is the thought that his splendid achievements—the romance of his whole career—will add to the glory and fame of Gray's Inn. And is his career not full of romance? I would say to Mr. Junior and the younger members of Hall that it is not necessary to the idea of romance that you should bolt to Gretna Green with the daughter of a multi-millionaire, and establish your fortune upon the exciting incident of a runaway marriage. It is true that another Lord Chancellor also from the Northern Circuit did something of the kind, and though in himself a most unromantic personality people talk of the romance of Eldon's life. No, Mr. Senior, great and eminent success in any walk of life, if associated with youth, contains the elements of romance, and we have in the life of our guest a union of brilliant success with youth, unique in the profession of the law.

I put on one side the case of a notorious personage—who in the evil days of the Stuarts was for a short season pitch-forked into power to do the dirty work of tyranny—I put Judge Jeffreys aside as one who was not in the line of the true apostolic succession of the Chancellors of England, and then I believe I am right in saying that our guest of to-night is the youngest man who has been called to the great office of Lord Chancellor of England. At the age of forty-six, when most men are fortunate if they have got their feet firmly established on the lower rungs of the ladder, at that age our guest is happily and comfortably installed on the very topmost rung of the ladder, and from that elevation—for who shall limit the possibilities of genius in this age?—from that great eminence he is now looking round for other worlds to conquer, like another famous young man who lived 2300 years ago.

Mr. Senior, this House, as you know, commissioned an eminent painter to paint the portrait of the Lord Chancellor. That portrait at the moment is in the Royal Academy. Its destined home is here, and it is intended that it shall hang as long as Gray's Inn lasts upon that wall near the portrait of the immortal Bacon. It is a great painting, but as a likeness it depicts him in his more pensive mood, as perhaps is only fitting in the case of the Chief Magistrate of the Realm clad in his robes of office. And it is in that grave and reverend—though appropriate—mood that he will go down to generation after generation of our successors in this Hall.

Mr. Senior, I can imagine your successor two hundred years hence in the company of some choice spirits, possibly of both sexes, seated in that very seat which you now occupy, drinking the ancient port of the Society, and immersed in those deep intellectual speculations which always distinguish the First Bar mess upon all occasions, and I can imagine one of your successor's messmates in a moment of forgetfulness—difficult to conceive, but possibly not wholly dissociated from the traditional potency of the Gray's Inn port when the fourth bottle is circulating—I can imagine him looking up to that wainscot and inquiring who was that grave and distinguished looking young man in gorgeous apparel looking down at him from the canvas. And then I can imagine your successor letting himself go and telling the whole great story, and saying: That is the youthful Lord Birkenhead, who was Lord Chancellor in the great days of King George V—because two hundred years hence they will call these days great days—that is the youthful Lord Birkenhead, who held great office in the days when everything that England had and stood for was put to the touch "to win or lose it all." The story of the young Chancellor, he will continué, is the romance of a young man who went up from a provincial town to Oxford and swept the board of every possible academical distinction, then went to the Bar of England—selecting with a degree of wisdom in which some of his contemporaries were wanting, Gray's Inn—and at the Bar at once won great and phenomenal success, who afterwards ventured upon the stormy sea of politics and in the House of Commons forthwith stepped into the front rank. And then I can imagine your successor possibly with an added note of pride in his voice, saying: When the testing time of the Great War came, in the anxious days of the autumn of 1914, this young man, then almost at the head of the Bar of England, making a princely income, cast £20,000 a year to the winds and himself went to the War. Called home for public duties, he entered upon the office of Attorney-General, filling it with eminent distinction and public advantage at the time when that office made more imperious demands upon the highest powers of mind and judgment of its holder than at any other period, and finally, beating all records at the age of forty-six, became Lord Chancellor of England. I think your successor will add one more sentence. When he became Lord Chancellor, though the one criticism upon his appointment had been that as he was a brilliant advocate he could not be a good lawyer—straightway he put that criticism to an open shame by taking his place at the head of the Judicature as though to the manner born, and within three short months by the universal testimony of the profession established a reputation as one of the greatest Judges who ever sat on the Woolsack.

Mr. Senior, I have only one word to add. Posterity in this Hall will look upon the Chancellor in his more pensive mood, but his contemporaries—we of this generation—have had the privilege of knowing him in his gayer moods. I will make bold to say that it is the man, the naturalness of the man, the gay and debonair spirit which fortune has not spoilt, which have endeared him to his comrades in this House, and which makes the celebration of to-night much more than the conventional recognition of a great success, makes it the heartfelt tribute of friends who have watched with sympathy and pride the irresistible sweep of his progress, and now the goal is reached, rejoice with him on a high position bravely fought for, honestly won, and now greatly filled.

The toast was drunk amid great enthusiasm, cheers being given for the Lord Chancellor and Lady Birkenhead.

THE LORD CHANCELLOR, on rising to reply, was received with further cheers and the singing of " For he's a jolly good fellow." He said : Mr. Senior. I do not know what life may have in store for me, but I know this, that, on its public side, it will afford no occasion which will fill me with a degree of emotion deeper than that which I experience as I address you to-night. Master Mattinson has proposed my health in language far too indulgent, but I am glad indeed that it should have been proposed on this occasion by one who is the sagacious custodian of our finances, and who has established a claim to gratitude so deep and permanent not only upon the present, but upon future generations of Gray's Inn men. Mr. Senior, I would wish to say in the first place, that while the present occasion is one to me of supreme personal interest, the principal significance of to-night, must in the eyes of history lie not in the extraordinary compliment paid to myself, it must lie in the long list, which you, sir, to-night read out of those members of this Society whose devotion to this House must be measured by the devotion which led them to die for their country.

Mr. Senior, they are not with us. They gave their brilliant youth to the country of which they were ornaments. The depth of our pride in them cannot be expressed in terms of rhetoric. Their names will live for ever in the history of this House, and as compared with them and what they did, or with the priceless unforgettable example which they have set, legal luminaries, believe me, are transient and undistinguished phantoms. Mr. Senior, the names of those members of this Society, the unconscripted members of Gray's Inn, men who in the supreme moment—for so I believe historians will pronounce it—the supreme moment of the fortunes of the British Empire, rushed to arms to defy and defeat a menace and challenge by the side of which the challenge of Philip of Spain, of Louis XIV and even of the great Napoleon were negligible—I say the names of those young men shall never be forgotten. In this House we can give them a special sanctuary, and we shall do it for all time, in our hearts. We shall also do what is much less important. We shall create a memorial, however unworthy, which will express for ever to posterity the measure of the debt which we owe to them, and the pride which we feel in their glorious sacrifice.

Mr. Senior, Master Mattinson has spoken of the Members of Parliament for Liverpool. His modesty led him to omit the circumstance that in the constituency for which I first sat in the House of Commons, I had a predecessor in Master Mattinson; and I am glad to add this, that his sound grasp of economy, to which this House is so much indebted, was not even in the early days forgotten by him, with the result that I succeeded to the least costly seat which any Member of the House of Commons ever filled. Master Mattinson has spoken to you to-night of those who before me have sat upon the Woolsack. He has spoken of the illustrious Bacon, Bacon who loved this House, Bacon who never forgot it in the days of his supreme and radiant prosperity, Bacon who, in the moment of his agony, crept here like a wounded animal to die, among those who, in spite of everything, loved and indeed worshipped him. Master Mattinson spoke also of Lord Brougham. I was left in some slight doubt as to the comparison which it was the object of our worthy colleague to establish in mentioning my poor name side by side with the names of those illustrious men. I am trying, as I always do, to look at these things in a detached way, and I am perhaps able to make an observation which is not disfigured by too much egotism. I think perhaps I have the advantage—it is the only advantage I claim—over the great Bacon, that I excel him in levity. I think in relation to Brougham that I may perhaps claim that I excel him in gravity. I desire to push neither comparison further.

We in this Inn are not likely to forget that he of the greatest brain which has ever been directed to jurisprudence, Bacon, proceeded from this House. There have been other great lawyers, great masters of the science of jurisprudence—a science which, among the giants, claims the highest qualities of the human brain—but never in my humble judgment has there been a man of law who attained so sublime a standard of intellectual quality in every department of human learning and science as Bacon.

Master Mattinson has spoken of old days. In recent years, we have been accustomed to address, not Mr. Senior, but Mr. Junior. I know not which practice is more correct, but I know for many years it has been the habit to address Mr. Junior. To-night we are told we must address Mr. Senior. I remember twenty-three years ago, when I was an undergraduate at Oxford, attending my first dinner in this Hall. I sat at that table, about five from the end, with my back to the wall. I was a Junior on that occasion, and very shortly after the Benchers had left the Hall—I recall this easily, because, so far as I remember, it was the last occasion upon which I addressed Mr. Senior in this Hall—I was incited to make the following request of Mr. Senior. The moment the Benchers withdrew, and at a period of the evening which I think was considered premature by those who at that time were responsible for the conduct and propriety of the Hall, I said: "Mr. Senior, may we smoke?" Mr. Senior, somewhat annoyed, said, "No, you may not." Unaccustomed to rebuffs of that kind, I rose and said, "Why not," upon which, your predecessor, having no suitable repartee ready, wisely remained silent. We were not allowed to smoke for a period which, I believe, was quite unusually prolonged in punishment of what was regarded as audacity in those days.

This recollection, as I have said, is twenty-three years old, and it leads me to remind you of the circumstances under which I first became a member of this House; it is indeed extremely agreeable to me that I should allow my memory to linger over those days, because it enables me, long after his death, to pay a tribute to the prescience of my father, whose example contributed much to my life, and whose wise counsel I think I may truthfully say I very seldom neglected. He was a member of the Middle Temple, and I remember when I was a boy sixteen years old, he said to me: "If I were able now to take my decision as between the various Inns of Court, I should not join the Middle Temple; I should join Gray's Inn." I was then a schoolboy of sixteen, and he explained to me why if he were making his choice again he would have chosen Gray's Inn. He said: "If you judge the Institution by beauty, it is the most beautiful of all the Inns of Court. It is the most intimate of all the Inns—and it is the smallest. It enables a man who relies not upon patronage, but upon his own ability to win advancement most swiftly." Mr. Senior, I had the great misfortune to lose my father when I was seventeen years old, and it did not fall to me to take the final choice as to which Inn of Court I should join for four or five years, by which time I was an undergraduate at the University of Oxford. Influenced only by the circumstance that it had been the advice of my father that I should join this House, I joined it, I suppose, about 1894, at a time when almost all my friends at Oxford were joining other Inns of Court.

Mr. Senior, I have always respected the wisdom of my father, but never, never did he give me more sagacious counsel, never did he give me counsel for which at this moment, nearly thirty years after his death, I thank him more than that which he gave me when he urged me to join this ancient House.

Mr. Senior, every ancient institution is certain in its history to undergo vicissitudes. At some moments it is a very great and powerful House; at others, it seems that it has fallen into nerveless hands, that the traditions of the past have been forgotten, and that no personalities adorn it at the moment who afford promise of an illustrious future. Our House, like other human institutions, has not been protected from those periods of anxiety and doubt, and I am not, I hope, disloyal to this Institution when I say that the moment when I happened to join it was not the most prosperous in its history. Mr. Senior, I look round to-night. I look at this distinguished assembly and I remember that crowded as this Hall is to-night, it has been necessary to appeal to the poll in order to select the occupants of at least sixty seats amongst those who listen to me. I look round on this Bench and I say, among friends, small as we are in numbers there is no Inn of Court which at this moment possesses a Bench more distinguished or more representative than ours, or which has contributed more to the fortunes of this Empire in the five years that have passed. Other Inns of Court are accustomed in their cups, and when no Gray's Inn men are present—I have seen these old men, before they make their vainglorious boasts, look round to see whether there is a Gray's Inn man present—to present extravagant and highly coloured pictures of the worthy societies which they see through such rosy glasses. At the Middle Temple they are even accustomed, so I am informed, though they never publish these fantastic and mendacious declarations, nor do they allow reporters to be present when they are made, to claim that their Hall is older than ours, and I am told that they have even glibly averred that their table was made of timber which came from a Spanish galleon, whereas, Mr. Senior, in a hackneyed phrase, every school-girl knows that in fact it was this table standing above which I address you to-night which was given as the planking of a Spanish galleon to this ancient House by a great benefactor—Queen Elizabeth of immortal memory—a Sovereign who dearly loved it, and honoured it by her frequent presence. We know well that if we look at the history of this House it can afford to challenge comparison by all the criteria by which men judge of the greatness of any legal institution, with any other of the Inns of Court. It is not for me to make too much of one circumstance, except that I think I can state that which I wish to state without excessive egotism, because I am assisted by an accidental circumstance. It might easily happen that another Inn of Court might produce a Lord Chancellor. In fact, in recent days there have been quite a number of Lord Chancellors. But at least this is certain, that no other Inn of Court can now produce two Lord Chancellors at the same time, and I greatly doubt whether there has ever been a moment at which it was possible for one Inn to produce on one and the same occasion the only two Lord Chancellors there are in the world. I may be allowed, I think, to add this—unless I have forgotten some of them, there are only five Lord Justices. Well, by a singular chance it happens that there are only four Inns of Court, and although the three other Inns of Court have each of them about three times as many members as we have, some, I believe four—that is their own claim, neither admitted nor denied—although that is so, by a singular chance it happens that out of the five Lord Justices two come from this small House. There being five Lord Justices to be distributed among four Inns of Court, if it were an early period of the evening, I would give you the precise mathematical calculation as to what in relation to our numbers we ought to be able to produce; but I merely say that there are four Inns of Court and we are the smallest of them all, and we have two. I think I need hardly remind you that of His Majesty's puisne judges, two of the most distinguished—one of old standing, Mr. Justice Lush, whose reputation as one of the most brilliant and persuasive advocates at the English Bar will not soon be forgotten by his contemporaries, and Mr. Justice Greer, for whose appointment I am glad to be responsible—are both members of this Society.

I am influenced by the mention of Mr. Justice Lush's name to refer to the days when not infrequently and much to my advantage he led me at the Bar, and am tempted to diverge into an estimate of the forensic qualities which led our friend, Mr. Justice Lush, to such extraordinary success. It is always a dangerous task to decide which of the qualities it is that lead any individual to forensic success, because, I suppose, there is none of us who has not said of such and such a man, "He is bound to succeed at the Bar," and after we have made most confidently such a prediction we almost always prove to be wrong, so uncertain and so incalculable are the rewards of the profession to which we belong or aspire to belong.

If I were to attempt to measure the forensic qualities which led Mr. Justice Lush to his acknowledged supremacy at the Bar of England—and I put on one side mere unimportant qualities such as a great knowledge of the law and great industry—I think that where the learned judge, if I may say so, always terrified me when I was his opponent was by his extraordinary and unmatched gift for tearful expression. If I was opposed to him, juries would say—you could almost hear them saying it—"Well, of course, F. E. Smith was the better advocate; he made much the better speech; his cross-examination was far abler, and his knowledge of the law more profound; but at the same time, the moment Mr. Lush got up you could see how deeply his client had suffered." I only add, as I do with deep sincerity, that, if I have allowed myself to make an observation in a spirit of levity about the learned judge, I venture on your behalf and on my own to assure him that there is no man in this Hall to-night who was not proud of his great career as an advocate, and who is not proud of his position to-day on the Bench.

Mr. Senior, I have this to add. I think I have for twenty-five years been a member of this Society, and I say, with deep sincerity, in every one of those years I have grown to love it more, and it has grown to play a larger part in my life. It is very difficult to appraise emotions or to assign degrees in a man's affections. There are his family, his friends, and then there are institutions. My family and my friends are near and dear to me; but when I come to institutions, much as I love my own college at Oxford, I say quite plainly that I know no institution which has played so great a part in my life, and which has made so profound and lasting an appeal to my allegiance and my affections, as this House within whose walls we sit to-night. I am persuaded, profoundly persuaded, of the destiny, worthy of its past, which awaits this Inn. We have had to struggle against every conceivable handicap, to which any Inn could be exposed. Our critics have advised young men to go to other Inns, which advice young men are increasingly disinclined to take. Our critics are accustomed to say that Gray's Inn is in a backwater; that we are remote from the Law Courts, away from the libraries; that Chambers are of no use in Gray's Inn. All these are formidable disparagements in the eyes of any man who intends to select an Inn, and it is perhaps the most striking proof of the greatness and individuality of this Inn that against all those disadvantages it has maintained its character and its individuality, and has developed its influence to a degree of which I say boldly in all its illustrious history that it has never equalled. I look forward to a future for this House even greater than its honoured past.

It is easy to find an argument founded upon pure materialism why a young man going to the Bar should choose Gray's Inn. Indeed, I can use a hundred against the suggestion that he should choose any other Inn. I say this in spite of its geographical inconveniences, in spite of its detachment, in spite of the fact that it lies in a backwater. I observe that in the last three months we have had more new members than at any similar period in the history of the Inn. I observe, too, that many of those new members are soldiers who are coming back from the War. Every week I have sent to me a list of the new members of this Society, and every week my feelings of pride grow when I realise of the new members who are coming to this Inn, that they will maintain and develop the greatness and tradition of this ancient House. What is it that in face of those admitted inconveniences leads young men to come to this Inn? I have no doubt as to the answer. I have no doubt that the very size of some of the other Inns of Court tends to foster an element of aloofness unfriendly to the esprit de corps without which no great institution can permanently flourish. We in this House have always clung to our corporate soul; we have always realised—to a degree never throughout the centuries equalled or even approached by other Inns of Court—the fellowship and the intimate atmosphere of collegiate life. We have been, and we are, a band of brothers. This I know well, that barristers dine here, and students dine here under circumstances in which neither barristers nor students ever dream of dining at other Inns of Court, and they dine here because they know they will meet their contemporaries, because they know they will meet those who grew up with them, who looked on life together with them through young eyes, in the days of its vernal spring. I drank to "The glorious immortal memory" * twenty-five years ago as they drink to-day. Shall I ever forget that I have drunk that toast within these historic walls? I am one of those who believe that this Inn will become the greatest of Inns. I understate the case. I am sure that we are the greatest Inn. We are incomparably the most beautiful. There is an intimacy and charm about this House which other Inns never rivalled and never can rival.

Let us be sure of our own destinies. Let us make up our minds, each according to the measure of his capacity, to realise this assurance, and to confront the adventure of life with this elementary proposition, that a Gray's Inn man is better than any other man; how much better he is, of course, may be made the subject of a long discussion. But a Gray's Inn man is better than any other man, he always has been better, he always will be better. Those whom I address inherit no mean kingdom. Younger men are listening. We have borne the burden of our day. We are entitled to say to you that we have borne it not unworthily. Some of us came here twenty years ago, some thirty, some fifty—our excellent acting Treasurer to-night was actually admitted a member of this Society five months before I was born!—and our part is nearly played. We have done it with all our hearts. We claim this boldly before you in the spirit of men who are entitled to say: Recognise what we have done. It is for you and your generation to take up the task which gradually, and in the necessity of things, must fall from our hands. It is for you to pursue the traditions which we have tried to understand and carry out. And if it be true that the result

* The reference is to the Toast of the "Pious, Glorious and Immortal Memory of Good Queen Bess," always honoured in Hall on Grand Nights.

of our exertions has been to place the Benehers of this House, and the Barristers of this House, and the Students of this House, in a position certainly of equality, perhaps even of ascendency—when the burden leaves us and our voices are still in death, it will fall to you to address yourselves to your task as men who love and reverence the Alma Mater as truly as we in our day loved and reverenced her.

MASTER LORD JUSTICE ATKIN said that he had a task that he was always ready to perform, viz. to propose the toast of the Students of Gray's Inn. They could not all be Lord Chancellors or Judges—he was not sure that all of them could be Barristers; Master Coward as Chairman of the Board of Studies presented certain obstacles not always easy to surmount—but they could at all events all be students. Those of them who were older and were Barristers looked back on their student days as the happiest days in their lives. It was then that they learned that love of the Inn and veneration for its customs and traditions which was the special characteristic of that House. He laid special emphasis on the importance of the rule which provided that men sat in Hall in order of seniority, and attributed to it in great measure the feeling of general good-fellowship which marked the corporate life of the Society. After dwelling on the change in the fortunes of the Inn that some of them had lived to see, and the great position which the Society now occupied, he assured his hearers that there was no Master of the Bench who would not readily afford what assistance he could to any student who came to him for advice. He proposed the health of the Students of Gray's Inn, and coupled with it the name of the Junior, Commander Chilcott.

LIEUTENANT-COMMANDER CHILCOTT, M.P., as Junior Student, responded and spoke of the pride with which the students of Gray's Inn regarded the proceedings of that night. He referred to the important part which Liverpool had played in producing the great men of England. Bacon had filled the position of Member for Liverpool, and the Lord Chancellor and Mr. Bonar

Law had recently been Members for Liverpool. One Master of that Bench had filled the seat in Liverpool which the Lord Chancellor had vacated, and the Junior Student of Gray's Inn who was addressing them now filled the same seat.

MASTER LORD JUSTICE DUKE said that the Treasurer had entrusted him with a toast which it was an honour to propose. He remarked that he ought to have been qualifying himself for it during many years, but the task had fallen to him unexpectedly, and he rose with some trepidation. He could remember no occasion in nearly forty years' experience of the Society—and he did not believe there ever was an occasion—when members of Gray's Inn were more proud of their membership than to-day. They had many inherited causes of satisfaction and some added reasons for pride in the present position of the Society. But underlying all this he thought that without question the great distinction of the Inn had been that it had attracted and held together from one generation to another not only able men, but companionable and lovable men. That had been the nature of their fellowship, and this had been their amiable dwelling. He asked them to drink to the health of " The Bar of Gray's Inn."

THE SENIOR IN HALL (Mr. A. H. Lush) briefly responded.

MASTER SIR JAMES CAMPBELL (LORD CHANCELLOR OF IRELAND) proposed the toast of " The Acting Treasurer " (Master Mulligan). He said one of the peculiarities of Gray's Inn had always been the genial welcome it had given to his fellow-countrymen from Ireland. He spoke with all sincerity when he said they were very conscious of this and very grateful. It had been a great pleasure for him to be there to-night to do honour to our Lord Chancellor. He had been associated with him for some years in political life and also at the Bar, and he would like to testify to his great esteem and admiration for him. He always thought one tremendous advantage he had was his great vitality. He would now ask them to drink to the health of the Acting Treasurer. He was a fellow-countryman of his. He had been a Master of the Bench for many years, and they all knew and appreciated his many services to the Society. No Bencher has shown a greater and more sincere interest in the welfare of the Inn, and he was proud to propose his health that night.

THE ACTING TREASURER briefly replied, and the proceedings terminated.

THE ARMISTICE—AND AFTER

NOVEMBER 17TH, 1918.

SERMON PREACHED IN THE CHAPEL ON THE SUNDAY AFTER THE ARMISTICE.

APRIL 18TH, 1920.

THE DEDICATION OF THE WAR MEMORIALS, INCLUDING THE SERMON PREACHED BY THE RIGHT REV. S. MUMFORD TAYLOR, D.D., BISHOP OF KINGSTON-ON-THAMES.

Henry Dixon & Son. London. Photogravure.

Gray's Inn Chapel – The Pulpit and Archbishops' Window.

THE END OF THE WAR

(A Sermon preached in Gray's Inn Chapel on Sunday, the 17th of November, 1918, by the Rev. R. J. Fletcher, D.D., then Preacher of the Society, now Canon Residentiary of Bristol Cathedral.)

"If the Lord Himself had not been on our side."—Psalm cxxiv. 1.

CAN we use this language? When the Kaiser spoke of God as his ally, and when his people spoke of "our good German God," we were revolted. Apart, too, from resentment at such presumptuous talk, we have realised, in connection with our study of the religious development of Israel, how the assumption of a national deity may survive the stage at which there is a deliberate belief in the existence of a plurality of gods, each with his chosen people, and how a narrow and arrogant view of the world and its destiny may result. Moreover, we have ideas on this subject which differ from those of our own fore-fathers—differ because of our greater knowledge of the history of the human race, and of the traces of its prehistoric development, and because of our greater knowledge as to the place of our earth in the universe. Our difficulty has been, perhaps, not to free ourselves from the assumptions made by Jew or German, but to conceive of the affairs of particular nations as having any great significance in the procedure of the universe, and in the Mind which directs that procedure.

If to-day we use the Psalmist's language, it will be in no boastful spirit engendered by a sense of national might; it will be with no assumption that ours is an arbitrarily chosen people with an exclusive racial claim upon Divine favour; it will be in some sense compatible with a due realisation of all that must be involved in a modern man's idea of the Divine majesty, that we use it.

But—shall we not use this language? Let us not assume that

only the marvellous, the mysterious, that which has no apparent adequate cause, exhibits the marks of Divine handiwork. What is marvellous to one generation is common-place to another. Everywhere there is law; everywhere also there is mystery. And God works in, and through, human brains and hands. Nor ought we to expect that a mechanical process of analysis can distinguish with precision between His work and men's.

But surely to-day we must needs be very strongly drawn to a conclusion that the great events of our time have their religious interpretation, that the careers of nations have a meaning in relation to one cosmic purpose which has underlain the whole long development of humanity on this planet! It is not the Christian contention that that cosmic purpose is for mankind here and now "the greatest happiness of the greatest number." The Christian view harmonises with that of the anthropologist that the purpose is for us the advance of spiritual life—intellectual, volitional, emotional. In that advance suffering, as well as pleasure, has its part to play. The Eternal Spirit who toils for our advance, suffers; the cross of Calvary is the symbol of that. We, as individuals, Churches, nations, are appointed to "suffer with Him, that we may be also glorified together." From the beginning man has been subject to pain and sorrow that he might grow in knowledge, in self-direction, in sympathy. "The creation groans and travails" in the generation of a more glorious life. Therein the sufferings of these four years have their place.

We are asked why we should thank God for the ending of the war, why He ever allowed it to begin and continue? I have spoken of various aspects of this question at various times of late. Let me say now that behind it is the question how there arose in Germany that rebellion against God, that idolatry which enthroned Might in the place of Right. These false moves of the human spirit are possible because of that measure of freedom which must be accorded if it is to grow. On the other hand, if the human spirit is to grow, its diseases must be healed; these false moves must needs be arrested and suppressed, though it be by terrible means. And the honest use of those means, and the efforts and the suffering they involve to the nation or nations called to be the Divine instrument of punishment and purgation, also have for that nation, or those nations, their virtue for spiritual growth. The end of the effort and suffering for them is also the occasion of completing an inward achievement. Who does not admit that, bleeding as our country is from the wounds of the conflict, tear-stained—but with proud tears—for the death of so many gallant sons, England stands to-day, greater, not only in power and prestige, but in wisdom and in character, than in the days before the gauntlet was thrown down, and she—reluctantly, in her unreadiness for battle, in her faith—took it up. For this we thank God.

But also " the Lord was on our side." I do not forget that, during the war, many of us had our moments of perplexity and gloom. There were moments when it seemed difficult to find a Christian interpretation of the course of things. Yet I think, even in the darkest hours of our fortunes, those of us who were not atheists felt that, whichever of our particular hopes might be disappointed, the War could not end in a German victory. We could not doubt that our country did right in drawing the sword. We could not doubt that to resist the German arrogance, the German idolatry of force, to resist the domination in Europe, or elsewhere, of a people so false and cruel, was to do, as a nation, the will of God, to further the Divine purpose for the race. Those of us who said so in those days knew that we only gave the due expression to what all the best of our countrymen, often inarticulately, felt. Faith is often wonderfully independent of theology; it was present, deep down, in many a mind to which the Church can but say wistfully, " *Utinam noster esses.*"

We were perplexed that we were so sorely tried—even though we recognised the purifying, redeeming, influence of the trial—perplexed that such gigantic sacrifices should be asked of us, perplexed as to the trend of events, as to the conclusion to which the great struggle was destined to lead.

Yet we endured. Surely it is no fancy, no obsolete thought, which we utter when we claim that the spirit of the nation was sustained by a Spirit greater than itself, by that Spirit whose power we trace in the high steadfastness of individual men and women, of the men who are pioneers of intellectual and moral movement, of all martyrs for truth and right, for Church or country; whose power we trace again in feminine self-sacrifice, in that maternal heroism and tenderness without which life in its higher phases, and especially human life, could not exist upon the earth. Surely the nation was inspired by the Mind which wills the spiritual progress of humanity, inspired because of that progress, inspired for the central cosmic purpose!

We claim no arbitrary choice of us, as of a grand vizier by an Oriental despot. Nor dare we say that we were favoured because of our righteousness. We have been inspired and sustained, not for ourselves alone, but for the right procedure of a great development, wherein the career of one nation—though it be prolonged through many centuries—is as the work of a week in the building of a cathedral. The victory won was needful that humanity might go forward, that a further stage might be reached and passed in that march of the human spirit whereof only recent features have any memorial in the chronicles of history. Therefore it was won. It will be in proportion as our Anglo-Saxon race sets itself to serve that great development that it will prosper in its victory, and taste the glory of those who, being led by the Spirit of God, are sons of God.

If it had not been that our cause was the cause of that development, "if the Lord Himself had not been on our side"! As we think to-day upon the number and equipment of our forces at the outbreak of the war; upon the mistakes and disasters of four years; upon the Russian betrayal of our trust and the Italian defeat; upon the submarine menace; upon the peril to us this last spring in France, and upon the clouded aspect of our future, which did not change till the fourth year of the conflict was complete—stoical as we are by temperament—must we not inwardly thrill with joyful gratitude that "the waters have not drowned us, nor the stream gone over our soul"? Can we refuse to thank God, who called us to this work, that, though the cost of achievement has been so terrible, it has been achieved? Can we refuse to say—as we think of the craft and might of the enemy we have overthrown—"Our help standeth in the name of the Lord, who made heaven and earth"?

"Thanks be to God who giveth us the victory!" Thanks

that He so inspired the peoples of our stock! Thanks that by His grace there were with us, in days thought to be days of decadence, so many men ready to endure hardship and danger, ready to face wounds and lifelong disablement, ready to lay down their lives in this cause!

The mind of the nation, I am sure, was expressed when in Gray's Inn Hall on Monday, at the call of the Treasurer, the head of the English Bar, the new-born joy in our victory, was at once associated with a simple act of reverence for the fallen. The members of this Society were not backward in springing to arms in the autumn of 1914. Thirty-seven * of them have made the great sacrifice. And as it has been with this and the other Inns of Court, so it has been with other seats of learning and with other professional associations. So it has been with the country at large. To God's gracious mercy and protection we commit our fallen brethren. Moreover, because of that which they have achieved for the world, and because of their fragrant memory, and because of the high example they have left to their generation and to posterity, we reject the thought that those young lives, even with all the seeds of promise which they showed, have in reality been wasted. It was a brief career that Jesus closed on Calvary. They have suffered with Him. They are glorified together.

Thanks be to God for them, and for their brethren in arms who survive! Thanks be to God that He was our refuge "when the blast of the terrible ones was as a storm against the wall"! Let it be said in this day of victory, "Lo, this is our God; we have waited for Him; we will be glad and rejoice in His salvation."

And let us face the future—its problems and perils—with that confidence in His ordering of human development which our victory should encourage. His purpose will go forward. Nothing that merely impedes it will endure. The message of the time to anxious patriots is "Lift up your hearts." Let their response be, "We lift them up unto the Lord."

* The final toll of the Fallen proved to be forty-four.

THE WAR MEMORIAL AND ITS DEDICATION

It was known at the time of the Armistice that thirty-nine members of the Society had fallen in the War, and the question of their Memorial within the precincts of the Inn was much in the minds of the Bench during the early part of the year 1919. There was general agreement that no better place could be found than the Chapel of the Society, and in June, 1919, Mr. M. W. Mattinson, K.C., one of the senior Masters of the Bench, informed his colleagues in a letter that he would " esteem it a privilege to bear the cost of a Memorial in the Chapel," and suggested that a Committee should confer with him as to the form which the Memorial might take.

The Bench accepted this offer on the 25th of June. A Committee was appointed with the Dean of the Chapel as Chairman, and a Barrister and a Student of the Society among its members. The Committee's first step was to seek the advice of Sir Reginald Blomfield, R.A., and Mr. Ernest Newton, R.A., on the questions of the appropriate position and the general form of the monument.

Both these gentlemen, who most courteously gave their services, agreed that a Memorial in stained glass in the centre window on the north side of the Chapel, and a sculptured stone Tablet on the south wall would provide a fitting monument and would dignify and adorn the Chapel.

Mr. Pomeroy, R.A.—the sculptor of the statue of Bacon erected by the Society in South Square in 1909—undertook the design and execution of the Tablet. The Window is the work of Mr. Christopher Whall. Both monuments are illustrated in this volume, but it may be convenient briefly to describe them.

The Window consists of three Lights. In the centre is placed the figure of St. Michael typifying victory over Evil. On the left is the figure of St. George. The Dragon lies slain between these two figures under the feet of each. Behind the head of St. George is shown a burning city typical of the destruction

Henry Dixon & Son, London, Photogravure.

Gray's Inn Chapel – The Victory Window.

wrought in the War. On the right is shown St. Louis of France representing our principal Ally. Above the head of that monarch appears the façade of the famous Sainte Chapelle erected during his reign. Below the figure of St. Michael is a panel in stained glass showing the ancient arch and bridge connecting Gray's Inn Hall with the Member's Common Room. The panel in the left-hand base, under the figure of St. George, bears the Union Jack. The right-hand base panel under the figure of St. Louis contains a shield of fleurs-de-lis. The inscription is as follows—

"A.M.D.G. ET IN PIAM MEMORIAM HUJUS HOSPITII SOCIORUM QUORUM NOMINA TABULA IN ADVERSA INSCRIPTA SUNT HANC FENESTRAM MILES WALKER MATTINSON DOMINI REGIS CONSIL EJUSDEM HOSPITII OLIM THESAURARIUS DEDIT."

The illustration on page 98 cannot even suggest the rich colour of the glass. The window has a north aspect, so that the artist was able to use his pigments without fear of over-emphasis. St. Michael is in silver armour, and above his head are golden rays. The Dragon at his feet is green. St. George stands in armour of gold with the Red Cross Shield and Banner, while St. Louis wears a cloak of rich deep blue on which are emblazoned the fleurs-de-lis in gold. Underneath the cloak is a garment of silver chain mail.

In order to place the memorial in the middle window of the Chapel it was necessary to remove a single Light which bore the figure of Lancelot Andrewes, Bishop of Winchester in 1590, and a member of Gray's Inn *honoris causa*. This window had been designed by Mr. Selwyn Image and erected under a bequest of Mr. H. C. Richards, K.C., M.P., a Bencher of the Inn who died in 1905 while serving in the office of Treasurer. The figure of Bishop Andrewes was therefore moved to one of the two side windows. In order to balance this figure and so provide a complete scheme of stained glass on that side of the Chapel, Mr. Mattinson presented another single Light window bearing a representation of Archbishop Sheldon to be erected in the other side window. Like Andrewes, the Archbishop was an honorary member of the Society, and an ancient glass panel bearing his coat of arms already occupied a part of the window where his figure now appears. The new Sheldon Window is the work of Professor Anning Bell, A.R.A.

The Monument on the other side of the Chapel is of Hopton-wood stone, ten feet in height, and bears the names of the members of the Inn, now known to be forty-four in number, whose Sacrifice is commemorated. Above these names is a piece of sculpture representing two Angels bearing a laurel wreath and crown with a riband on which appear the words, "Their name liveth for evermore." Underneath the names runs the following inscription :—

"TO THE MEMORY OF FORTY-FOUR GALLANT GENTLEMEN, MEMBERS OF THE HONOURABLE SOCIETY OF GRAY'S INN, WHO AT THEIR COUNTRY'S CALL LAID DOWN THEIR LIVES IN THE GREAT WAR—1914–1918."

All these works were completed and in position by April, 1920, and on Sunday morning, the 18th of April, a special Service was held in the Chapel to commemorate the Fallen and to dedicate their monument.

The Masters of the Bench present at the Service were: The Treasurer (Mr. Montagu Sharpe, K.C.); The Lord Chancellor (The Right Hon. Lord Birkenhead); Mr. M. W. Mattinson, K.C.; Sir Lewis Coward, K.C.; Mr. C. A. Russell, K.C.; Mr. T. Terrell, K.C.; The Right Hon. Lord Justice Duke; Mr. Herbert F. Manisty, K.C.; Mr. Edward Clayton, K.C.; Mr. Arthur E. Gill; Mr. E. F. Vesey Knox, K.C.; The Right Hon. Lord Justice Atkin; The Right Hon. Sir William Byrne, K.C.V.O., C.B.; The Hon. Mr. Justice Greer; Mr. C. Herbert-Smith.

The body of the Chapel was filled by members of the Society and relatives of those whose names appear on the tablet.

The Lord Bishop of Kingston-on-Thames (The Right Rev. Samuel Mumford Taylor, D.D.) dedicated the War Memorials and preached the Sermon. His Lordship was accompanied by the Rev. Harold Mattinson, M.A., who acted as Bishop's Chaplain, and the Rev. J. L. Phillips, B.D., the Reader of the Society.

The Service opened with the singing of the Hymn, " For all the Saints who from their labours rest." This was followed by Morning Prayer read by The Reader. The Dean of the Chapel (Sir Lewis Coward, K.C.), read the First Lesson, which was taken from the Book of Ecclesiasticus (XLIV, v. 1–14), beginning with the well-known passage, " Let us now praise famous men and our Fathers that begat us." The Second Lesson (Revelation VII, v. 9–17) was read by the Lord Chancellor.

After the Second Lesson the Choir sang the anthem, " Comes, at times, a stillness as of even." The gentle spirit of Oakeley's music, heard at its best in the small chapel and beautifully rendered by the Organist (Mr. Charles Long) and the Choir, made this anthem a fitting prelude to the Service of Dedication which immediately followed.

The two dedicatory prayers offered by the Bishop were as follows:—

Dedicatory Prayer for Window

Almighty and Everlasting God, who art the Father of Lights, from whom cometh down every good and perfect gift, whose Son our Lord Jesus Christ was that Light which lighteth every man that cometh into the world, we humbly beseech Thee to accept, bless, and hallow this Window which we now dedicate to Thy Glory and the adornment of this Thy Holy House in loving and pious memory of those Members of this Society who fell in the War, and grant that all who look upon it with true faith in Thee may so endeavour to adorn their lives with the beauty of holiness that, being enlightened by Thy grace they may, with these Thy Servants, be counted worthy to find a place in Thy Temple in Heaven, through Jesus Christ our Lord. *Amen.*

Dedicatory Prayer for Memorial Tablet

Almighty and Everlasting God, we humbly beseech Thee to accept, bless, and hallow this Monument, dedicated to Thy

Glory, and in loving and pious memory of those whose names are thereon inscribed. Grant that as many as look upon it may be likewise led to a life of love and sacrifice here, and that, hereafter, we may all, with these Thy servants, be counted worthy to enter upon our heavenly inheritance through Jesus Christ our Lord. *Amen.*

After the dedicatory prayers the Dean of the Chapel read the names of the Members to whom the Window and Tablet had been dedicated, while the whole congregation stood. The hymn " How bright these glorious spirits shine " was then sung, and at its conclusion the Bishop of Kingston preached the dedicatory sermon.

It will be seen that the address contained passages which carried it beyond its immediate purpose—great as that purpose was—and made it appropriate as the final expression of the Society's sense of loss, its effort and achievement during the War.

The Bishop's text was taken from I St. Peter II, 21, " Christ also suffered for us, leaving us an example, that ye should follow his steps." The Bishop proceeded :—

We have come to dedicate a memorial, and it is a memorial of suffering. The Epistle appointed for the day accords well with that. It points to the suffering of God Incarnate for us, and speaks of it as " an example, that ye should follow his steps." True, his suffering was unique as was his Person. All effort to bring that on to the plane of an unselfish life, ending in a willing martyrdom, and no more, fails. We feel that it does not go deep enough. Something more lies behind the fact, as Sir Oliver Lodge has put it, that " at the foot of the cross there has been a perennial experience of relief and renovation," for it has satisfied the " sense of impotence, of the impossibility of achieving peace and unity in one's own person, a feeling that aid must be forthcoming from a higher source." So the distinguished man of science puts it, and so the simpler soul assents :—

" All for sin could not atone
Thou must save, and thou alone."

But though his suffering, who taketh away the sin of the world, stands apart in its significance, the example remains. So he himself said, " If any man will come after me, let him deny himself, and take up his cross, and follow me." And in words which would sound strangely had not familiarity turned their edge, St. Paul speaks of " filling up on his part that which is lacking of the afflictions of Christ," and of his life being " poured out as a libation," in sacrifice.

It is one of the facts of life that we come to recognise with the years how labour and pain for the sake of others, part voluntary, part involuntary, runs through the whole of human life. We only live through the service of others; and in turn we serve our fellows. " Sacrifice," it has been said, " sacrifice alone is fruitful;" whether it seems to be a waste, a failure, or not.

Certain it is that our hearts answer to it, whenever and wherever we find it. Alas! for our blindness, that it is sometimes right under our eyes, and we don't see it. But when we do, it lifts us up. It tells us of high possibilities in this human nature that often looks, and is, so mean. Whether it be the surgeon, who loses his finest instruments, his hands, in dauntless persevering research; or the little servant-girl we remember in the Borough, who saved the children in her care from the flames of the burning house at the cost of her own life; or the young officer of the Antarctic expedition, who stepped out into the tempest, the murderous cold and the dark, saying that he " might be some time," to give his comrades a better chance of life—the appeal never fails. Or, coming to our thoughts to-day, the stories that have dimmed our eyes from the fields of Flanders and of France, these few years past—that bridge which must be destroyed before the enemy's advance, and one man after another goes forward to fire the charge, shot down before he reaches it, another quietly taking his place till the twelfth achieved it, and himself dropped dead. No fuss, no heroic pose; only the sacrifice made for country, for the rest. Wherever it be, it is the noblest thing we have. The most appealing of all chords to strike is that of self-sacrifice.

It sounds here to-day. One of the members of your Society has desired the privilege of setting up in this sacred place a memorial—and it is indeed a fitting and beautiful one—of the forty-four men, members of Gray's Inn, who laid down their lives in the Great War. That is the toll of death. It does not represent the sum of suffering. On the outbreak of the War the response was immediate. Out of the ninety-eight students keeping term and eligible for service, seventy-four were serving before the end of the year. But that was not all. Others returned from Canada, Australia, Africa, Burma, China—some four hundred in all. Benchers, Barristers, Students, went to swell the great torrent of life pouring from every part of the Empire and turned upon the field of battle—soldiers not by calling, but for their country's sake—not all to return. The names on the memorial are eloquent. "They represent" (I quote the words of the Dean of your Chapel) "every class. One of them, a 2nd Lieutenant, bore a name greatly honoured in English legal history, and in the roll of membership of this Inn, the name of Romilly. Another, his contemporary, began life as clerk in a barrister's chambers. He died a Major, having first won the Military Cross for conspicuous gallantry in action. Each of them held the same scholarship here, and each was on the threshold of a career of great promise. The graves of this devoted company are scattered widely—in France and Belgium, in Egypt and Italy, in Mesopotamia, East Africa, and the North Sea. One of them fell on the deck of the boat he commanded at Zeebrugge."

In the sixteenth century, and at a time when Gray's Inn was the first in importance of the Inns of Court, it was said that they were "the noblest nurseries of humanity and liberty in the kingdom." * The members of this Inn have not belied the tradition of the centuries. May the memorial before us help in the years to come to keep the memory green of these brave men, as by those who knew and loved them their memory is cherished to-day.

We follow them in thought out of sight, beyond the veil, with prayer that God will bring them always nearer to himself. Let us never think of them as unconscious, as lost to love and thought and care for us, but as alive. Though the gulf seems

* Ben Jonson, in the dedication of "Every man out of his Humour."

to us so awfully deep, the veil so impenetrable, there is no separating line, no veil, in the Divine sight, between the living and those whom we call " dead," for " all live unto him."

> " We call them dead,
> But they look back and smile
> At our dead living in the bonds of flesh,
> And do rejoice that in so short a while
> Our souls shall slip the leash."

Not all saints, but all souls, and every one in the hands of God, by a baptism of blood.

I said that we came to dedicate a memorial of suffering. It is so, and we are not to forget it, or we fail in gratitude. Not the garnering of those who having served their generation through long years have fallen quietly asleep, but those who were in the fulness of life, or standing on its threshold; precious in his sight of whom we sometimes forget that which the familiar hymn, in its original form, expressed telling of " the wondrous cross, on which the young prince of glory died." Like the costly offering once poured out on his feet, the perfume of it fills all the house. All over the land, as here this morning, are those who knowing how gallantly it was given, are sad with a proud sorrow for those who flung into the treasury, with both hands, all that they had.

But we come to dedicate the memorial of victory as well. It was not a waste, not all a wild pathetic mistake, a failure. The steps of suffering they followed, consciously or unconsciously, were steps that led to victory. Eastertide, still with us, brings the message of the victor over sin and death. " Fear not; I am he that liveth, and was dead, and behold I am alive for evermore." His victory the assurance of ours. " Peace be unto you."

Victory is the note struck by the window that has added to the adornment of this historic spot. It shows us Michael, the warrior archangel, guardian of Israel, with the tranquil assurance of a power that belongs to the messenger of the Lord of Hosts: the angel of the Presence, through whom it was believed that the tables of the law were given. And St. Louis, King of France—France at war with England in his day, but in the

Great War an ally—the Crusader of the thirteenth century, and one, moreover, who gave to his people a new judicial organisation, a better administration of justice. And George, the young soldier of the early days of Christianity, whose name rang out at Cressy, "St. George for England," the martyr who stands for the Empire's chivalry; stands as the ideal of those spiritual unseen forces, a great cloud of witnesses, who watch the conflict of the powers of good and evil with absorbing interest, and it may well be have power to nerve and cheer, strangely as it may sound to the materialised thought that wraps us round:—

> "Strong servant of the God who gave
> His angels charge concerning us."

This memorial is meant to stir more than grateful remembrance and prayer in those who see it; it is to be an inspiration. Their sacrifice helped others to carry things through to a victorious end. But its inspiration should extend beyond that, and be a force impelling us to do our best, as they did, for our country. There are changes to be faced that challenge a mass of prejudice, of custom, of selfishness. Can we hope to face them without catastrophe? There is no assurance of that whatever save in God, who giveth the victory, under whose hand things make for righteousness, whose vast Fatherhood is the only real and lasting foundation for the brotherhood of man, and is wrapped about all his children, patiently. But we are not mere passive spectators of a "Providence." God works through us; expresses himself through us, individually and corporately. There is a "moral equivalent of war." Archbishop Laud looks down from his window here, and we think how manfully he suffered and died for his Church and King. But after him Sheldon, to whose work and character scant justice has often been done, reminds us how it fell to him, though nurtured in the same absolutist school, to rebuke the king for whom he too had laboured, to refuse him the Sacrament because of the scandal of his life, and to lose his favour. And was it not the harder part to witness by life than by death? That is a parable of the call that comes to us. If it is a great thing and a glorious to die for the right, it is also a glorious thing, and the strain is longer if not sharper, to live for it.

We live in greater days than any on which we look back as epoch-making times. Our danger is to under-estimate their significance, and so to fail in a sense of our trust. They are days in which the only faith, the hope, the love, that we have seen in Christ, the revealer of God, only that, reflected in human life, can save the world. We have seen a victory that came with clashing bells, and the roll of the organ, the tramp of strong men, and the thunder of welcoming cheers, and we have given thanks. We long to-day for a victory that is deeply laid in surrendered wills, and changed hearts, " the sacrifices of God," who giveth the victory, that is through Jesus Christ our Lord.

After the Benediction buglers of the Welsh Guards sounded " The Last Post," and a very affecting Service ended with the singing of the National Anthem.

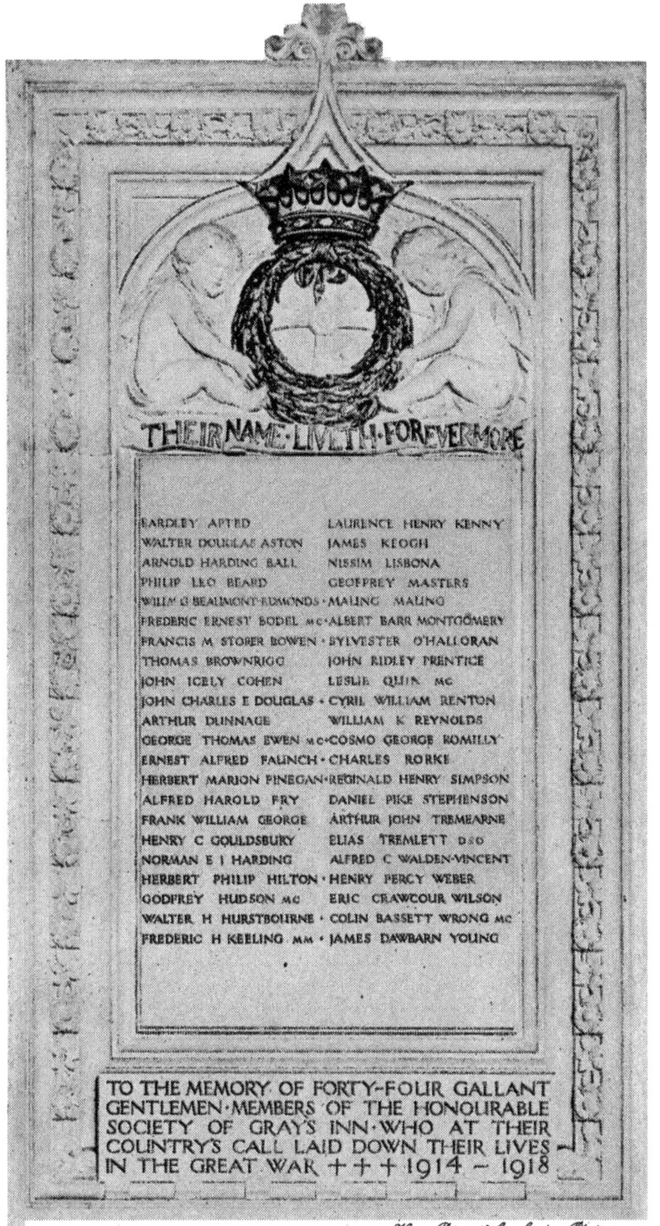

Henry Dixon & Son, London. Photogravure.

Gray's Inn Chapel.
The Memorial to Fallen Members.

THE ROLL OF HONOUR

SHORT MEMOIRS OF MEMBERS OF GRAY'S INN WHO WERE KILLED IN ACTION OR DIED ON ACTIVE SERVICE

LIEUTENANT EARDLEY APTED was educated at Cranleigh School, and called to the Bar in 1913. On the outbreak of war he joined the Inns of Court O.T.C. as private. He was first commissioned to the 9th Queen's (Royal West Surrey) Regiment and then to the 11th Battalion in France. He was killed on the 31st of July, 1917, in the trenches at Zillebeke, being struck by a bullet in the forehead, after having been slightly wounded earlier in the day. His Colonel described him as an officer "who commanded his company with quite remarkable skill, his powers of organisation being quite marvellous." He was thirty-three years of age.

CAPTAIN WALTER DOUGLAS ASTON was educated at New College, Worthing, and at London University. He became Foundation Scholar of Downing College, Cambridge. He was awarded the Whewell Scholarship for International Law, and became Fellow of Downing, and afterwards held there the offices of Steward, Librarian, and Lecturer in Law. He was called to the Bar in 1910. He joined the forces in April, 1915, receiving his commission as Second-Lieutenant in the 2/1st Cambridge Regiment, being promoted Captain in 1917. He was mortally wounded on the 1st of November, 1917, when gallantly leading his men, in the face of heavy shelling, in an attack on the German trenches. He died in hospital on the following day at the age of thirty-five. A brother officer described him as one "whose example of living was of the highest, and whose influence was that of a Christian gentleman in the very best sense of the word."

LIEUTENANT ARNOLD HARDING BALL was the third son of the late W. E. Ball, LL.D., also a barrister of Gray's Inn. He was educated at the City of London School, and was called to the Bar in 1910. He received his commission in the 5th (Cinque Ports) Battalion, Royal Sussex Regiment (T.F.) on the 30th of December, 1915, and went to the front on the 30th of September, 1916, remaining in the fighting area on the Somme and in Flanders until the 9th of April, 1918, when he was killed while on duty in the trenches by a German shell. He was twenty-nine years of age.

LIEUTENANT PHILIP LEO BEARD was called to the Bar in 1909, and practised at Birmingham until 1914, when he received his commission in the Royal Warwickshire Regiment. He died of wounds received on active service in France on the 9th of September, 1916, being then thirty-four years of age.

SECOND-LIEUTENANT WILLIAM GEORGE BEAUMONT BEAUMONT-EDMONDS was called to the Bar in 1909. On the 2nd of September, 1914, he enlisted as a private in the Queen's Westminster Rifles, and in 1915 received the King's Commission as Second-Lieutenant in the 22nd County of London Regiment. He proceeded to France, and on the 17th of September, 1916, was killed in action at High Wood, near Longueval, by an enemy shell exploding in the trenches where he was setting a splendid example to his men during a severe bombardment. He was then thirty-three years of age.

CAPTAIN FREDERIC ERNEST BODEL, M.C., was a graduate in Laws of the Victoria University, Manchester, and was called to the Bar in 1908.

In September, 1914, he received his first commission in the 8th (Irish) Battalion Liverpool Regiment as Second-

Lieutenant, being subsequently promoted Captain. He served also in France in the Trench Mortar Battery of the 55th Division, and was awarded the Military Cross "for bravery when in command of his battery in the front line." He was killed in action on the 31st of July, 1917, at the age of thirty-six.

LIEUTENANT FRANCIS MOULL STORER BOWEN was educated at Brentwood School, and became an undergraduate of London University. He joined the 9th Battalion Royal West Kent Regiment in 1914 as Second-Lieutenant, and was later transferred to the 1st Battalion Inniskilling Fusiliers, serving in Egypt from January 1916. He was later drafted to France, where he was seriously wounded on the 1st of July, 1916, in the severe fighting at Beaumont-Hamel, most of his comrades being killed or wounded. He was reported to be missing, his death not being confirmed until later. He was thirty-two years of age, having been called to the Bar in 1908. He was one of four brothers who served in the war.

LIEUTENANT THOMAS BROWNRIGG was educated at Belvedere College, Dublin, and was admitted as a student at Gray's Inn in 1913. In 1915 he joined the Inns of Court O.T.C. as a private, and was gazetted Second-Lieutenant in the 15th Middlesex Regiment, with which unit he served in France from May 1916 to February 1917, when he joined the Royal Flying Corps. He served in France as a pilot for nine months, being shot down twice in one day. He returned home to recover from his injuries, and was then engaged in instructional work in England, where he was drowned when flying on active service on the 21st of August, 1918. His machine crashed during foggy weather in the sea off Southbourne. He was one of three brothers, all with meritorious war records. He was twenty-eight years of age.

CAPTAIN JOHN ICELY COHEN was educated at Bradfield College and Queens' College, Cambridge. In September, 1914, he was gazetted Second-Lieutenant in the East Lancashire Regiment, and was subsequently promoted Captain in the 12th Devon Regiment. He served in 1915 in the Ypres fighting, his battalion being almost wiped out. Having recovered from shell-shock, he again returned to France in 1916, and was mortally wounded on the 11th of August, 1917, by a German shell near Poperinghe, Ypres. Before losing consciousness, he recommended for notice the assistance given to him by one of his men who had endeavoured to rescue him. He was reported to be a very reliable and considerate officer. He was admitted as a student of Gray's Inn in 1915, and was twenty-five years old.

MAJOR JOHN CHARLES EDWARD DOUGLAS was educated at Radley and Merton College, Oxford. He was called to the Bar in 1900, and was in considerable practice at Shanghai, which he gave up when war was declared, and left with a contingent in November, 1914, for home. He received a commission as Captain in the 10th Battalion Yorkshire Regiment, and after nine months training proceeded to France. He came safely through the heavy fighting at Loos in October, 1915, when all his senior officers were killed. He was then promoted Major, but on the 18th of December, 1915, when going the rounds with his sergeant, was picked off by a German sniper hidden in a chimney-stack and killed. He was thirty-nine years of age.

SECOND-LIEUTENANT ARTHUR DUNNAGE was admitted as a student in 1911. He was educated at Fauconbridge and Woodbridge Schools and Merton College, Oxford. He enlisted in 1914 in the Public Schools Battalion of the Royal Fusiliers, and was first commissioned in May, 1915, in the 3rd Battalion Rifle Brigade. He went out to France

Mentioned in P217 of –
Andrew R. Buxton, Rifle Brigade

in November, 1915, and was killed on the 1st of September, 1916, when leading his company into action, being then twenty-five years of age.

CAPTAIN GEORGE THOMAS EWEN, M.C., was educated at Manchester Grammar School. He acted as a Barrister's clerk for some years in Manchester. Subsequently he was called to the Bar at Gray's Inn in 1913. He received a commission in October, 1914, as Second-Lieutenant in the 3rd Manchester Regiment, and was afterwards transferred to the 1st Manchesters in France. He fought at Neuve Chapelle, and was mentioned in despatches for distinguished bravery in the field. He took part in further engagements, including the second Battle of Ypres, and was awarded the Military Cross for having, "near Ypres on 26th April 1915, after the machine-gun officer was wounded, taken charge of the guns and displayed great gallantry and resource in collecting them under heavy fire, and bringing them into action, which materially assisted in holding the line gained." In December, 1915, he was sent to Mesopotamia with the Indian forces, and took part in several battles. On the 8th of March, 1916, he was killed at Es. Sinn, being severely wounded when in the trenches, and then ordering his men to save themselves when they offered to help him. Captain Ewen was a well-known mountaineer and member of the Alpine Club, and a fearless leader of men. He was thirty-seven years of age when he fell in action.

SECOND-LIEUTENANT ERNEST ALFRED FAUNCH was educated at Parmiter School and became a Higher Division clerk of the Local Government Board. He was called to the Bar in 1908. In December, 1915, he enlisted as a cadet in the Royal Garrison Artillery, and was promoted Second-Lieutenant in the 112th Battery in 1916. He was killed in action on the 4th of May, 1917, near Angres, France, at the age of thirty-seven, and rests in Lieven Communal cemetery.

CAPTAIN HERBERT MARION FINEGAN was educated at Stonyhurst, and at the University of Liverpool, where his record was brilliant, for he won every Law prize, including the University Law Scholarship. He was an ardent and capable Irish Nationalist, and Vice-President of the Irish Society in Liverpool. He was President of the Guild of Undergraduates, and holder of the University Championships for the half-mile, mile and two miles. He entered as a student at Gray's Inn in 1913, and gained the Bacon Scholarship of the Society. He was a subaltern in the 8th (Irish) Territorial Battalion King's Liverpool Regiment, when war commenced, and was promoted Captain in 1914. He went to France in 1915 with his unit. On the 16th of June, 1915, he led his men in an attack upon trenches occupied by Prussian Guards at Festubert, saying, "Come on, Irish, let us show what we can do," and was there immediately shot, dying a few moments afterwards, "leaving to his race an imperishable glory and an everlasting inspiration of noble and heroic deeds." He had prophesied that he would either go home with a Victoria Cross, or stay in France with a wooden one, and he kept his word. He laid down his life for his country at the age of twenty-four.

SECOND-LIEUTENANT ALFRED HAROLD FRY was educated at Harrow and King's College, Cambridge, where he was Foundation Scholar. He was 16th wrangler in 1917. He was in the Inns of Court O.T.C. when war broke out, and in 1914 received his commission in the 22nd London Regiment (The Queen's). He was drafted to France in December, 1915, and on the 10th of October, 1916, was severely wounded during the battles of the Somme, dying in hospital at Le Touquet on the 30th of October, 1916, aged thirty years. He was called to the Bar in 1912.

SECOND-LIEUTENANT FRANK WILLIAM GEORGE was called to the Bar in 1913. When War broke out he enlisted in the 6th Battalion Gloucester Regiment, and was later commissioned to the 5th Battalion Dorset Regiment, which he accompanied to Gallipoli in July, 1915. He was killed on that peninsula on the 22nd of August, 1915, aged thirty-four years.

CAPTAIN HENRY CULLEN GOULDSBURY was a Native Commissioner and Justice of the Peace in Northern Rhodesia. He was admitted a student in 1912. He joined the King's African Rifles in 1915 and died, early in 1916, on active service. He was thirty-four years of age.

LIEUTENANT-COLONEL NORMAN ERNEST JASPER HARDING, M.B., studied at University College, Liverpool, and graduated at Edinburgh University. He entered the Royal Army Medical Corps in 1901, and was seriously wounded in the Boer War. He went to France with No. 12 General Hospital on the outbreak of War in 1914, and served there until 1916, when he took his unit to India. He died of cholera on active service at Colaba Military Hospital on the 10th of August, 1916, when forty-one years of age. He was admitted as a student of Gray's Inn in 1911.

CAPTAIN HERBERT PHILIP HILTON was educated at Malvern College, and was admitted as a student in 1907. He had served in Robert's Horse throughout the Boer War, and in 1900 was given a commission in the 3rd Middlesex Regiment by Lord Roberts. He rejoined the Army shortly after the outbreak of War, and was killed in action in Belgium on the 16th of February, 1915.

MAJOR GODFREY HUDSON, M.C., was educated at Victoria College, Jersey, and Trinity College, Cambridge. In September, 1914, he enlisted in the Inns of Court O.T.C. and obtained a commission in the 6th Battalion Royal West Kent Regiment in November, 1914. In 1916 he was transferred to the Machine-Gun Corps, being promoted Captain in 1917, and Major in 1918. In 1915, before going to France, he was bracketed equal for the Richards prize at Gray's Inn. On the 4th of August, 1916, he was awarded the Military Cross "for conspicuous gallantry during operations. He carried out a dangerous reconnaissance with two other officers, who were both killed. He advanced to the enemy's trenches in front of a captured position, and brought back valuable information."

During the fierce enemy advance on the 12th of April, 1918, Hudson led his Machine-Gun Company forward near Doulieu. Only a few men, but no officers, returned. He was instantaneously killed, having again displayed magnificent courage. His body was never found. He was only twenty-four years of age when he fell. He kept up his legal studies during the War, taking his text-books with him wherever he went, smuggling them, for the purpose of study, into the limber of his gun-carriage at night. He was admitted as a student in June, 1914, and there is little doubt that his legal career would have been as remarkable as his military history.

SECOND-LIEUTENANT WALTER HIRSCH (HIRSCHBEIN) HURSTBOURNE was educated at the City of London School, where he had a brilliant career. He obtained an open scholarship at St. John's College, Oxford. In 1910 he was admitted a student of Gray's Inn. He was on the staff of *The Daily Mail* in 1913, and afterwards on *The Times*. In June, 1915, he joined the Inns of Court O.T.C. He received his commission in the 4th Wessex Brigade Royal Field Artillery, and was drafted to France in November, 1916. He was killed in action at Wytschaete on the 23rd of June, 1917, while doing observation work as "liaison" officer to his battery. He was then thirty years of age. His Commanding Officer described him as "a model officer, whose military future was assured. His charming personality and great literary gifts made him most popular," and "his death was a distinct loss to the unit and to the Army."

SERGEANT-MAJOR FREDERIC HILLERSDON KEELING was educated at Winchester and Trinity College, Cambridge, where he obtained First Class Honours in the History Tripos. He was a founder of the Cambridge University Fabian Society and an active politician. He was admitted as a student at Gray's Inn in 1907, but was never called to the Bar. At the outbreak of War he was Assistant Editor of *The New Statesman*. He enlisted in August, 1914, in the 6th Duke of Cornwall's Light Infantry, and became Sergeant-Major of the Grenadier Company. He was awarded the Military Medal in 1916. He was killed on the 18th of August, 1916, by a German sniper when leading a bombing charge along a German trench in Delville Wood. His Commanding Officer said that "he did magnificently in the fight, and the party he was leading did particularly valiant work; he was one of the bravest of men. His influence and brilliance were felt throughout the battalion, for he was an immense factor for good among the non-commissioned ranks, and a link between officers and men. Three times he was asked to take a commission, but he always refused, replying that he thought he was doing more useful work where he was." He was thirty-one years of age when he fell in action.

SECOND-LIEUTENANT LAURENCE HENRY KENNY was educated at the City of London School, being called to the Bar in 1911. In September, 1914, he joined the Inns of Court O.T.C. and was gazetted Second-Lieutenant in the 8th Battalion Suffolk Regiment in December, 1914. He was drafted to France in December, 1915, and was reported missing after a midnight trench raid on the 25th of June, 1916, at Suzanne de Bray, near Cambrai, being then thirty-four years of age.

CAPTAIN JAMES KEOGH was educated privately and at St. Charles' College, Kensington, being called to the Bar in 1903. He was a District Auditor of the Local Government Board. In January, 1915, he joined the 3rd Home Counties Field Ambulance as Hon. Lieutenant and Quartermaster, and was promoted Captain in 1916. He served in France and Salonica, being four times mentioned in despatches. He died in January, 1919, on active service, at Batoum, aged forty.

PRIVATE NISSIM LISBONA was educated at the Manchester Grammar School and Manchester University, where he graduated as M.A. He was called to the Bar in 1908, and practised in Manchester until September, 1914, when he joined the 20th (Public Schools) Battalion Royal Fusiliers. He went to France in 1915, and served in the trenches. Later he became attached to the headquarters of the Royal Engineers for legal duties. In July, 1916, he rejoined his battalion, at his own request, and took part in the engagement at High Wood. He was afterwards posted as missing with a large number of other officers and men. His body was found later and buried. He was thirty-four years of age.

LIEUTENANT GEOFFREY MASTERS was educated at Colfe Grammar School, and was subsequently in the service of the Commercial Union Assurance Company, being called to the Bar in June, 1914. At the outbreak of War he was a private in the London Scottish Battalion, and went out with his unit to France in September, 1914. He was invalided home at Christmas, 1914, and having recovered, was commissioned in February, 1915, to the 9th Royal Fusiliers, and became an instructor of snipers. He was killed by rifle-fire while leading his company in an attack near Arras on the 9th of April, 1917. His Colonel wrote: "He was one of the best officers we had, and a fine example of manliness and cheerfulness to his men at all times."

PRIVATE MAUNG MAUNG, a native of Burma, was admitted as a student in 1911. In 1916 he voluntarily enlisted in the 18th Battalion London Regiment (London Irish Rifles) and served in France in the Battles of the Somme. He was discharged as medically unfit after some months' duty in the trenches, and then returned to Burma, where he was employed in recruiting work. He was accidentally drowned when on duty in August, 1917, being then twenty-six years of age.

CAPTAIN ALBERT BARR MONTGOMERY was educated at Perth High School, Australia, and subsequently became an undergraduate of London University, being admitted as a student at Gray's Inn in 1914. In July, 1915, he joined the Inns of Court O.T.C. as a private, and received the King's Commission in September, 1915, in the 1/7th Worcester Regiment. He went to France with his battalion in March, 1916, and was promoted Captain just before he was severely wounded by shrapnel when leading his company in an attack on concrete blockhouses at Alberta Farm, St. Julien, near Ypres, on the 17th of August, 1917. He died, at the age of twenty-five, in hospital at Vlamerlinghe. He was mentioned in despatches in November, 1917.

CAPTAIN SYLVESTER NORTH EAST O'HALLORAN, who had volunteered as a private in the South African War in 1900, joined the 9th Essex Regiment as Lieutenant in December, 1914, and served as Area Commandant in France, being promoted Captain in 1916. He was killed at the age of forty-nine, at Monchy-le-Preux, on the 9th of August, 1917, when gallantly leading his company across the German wire entanglements, his last words being: "Go for it, boys, when the barrage lifts," his company being terribly cut up in the advance. He was educated at Cranleigh School, and was called to the Bar in May, 1912.

SECOND-LIEUTENANT JOHN RIDLEY PRENTICE, an undergraduate of the University of London, was admitted as a student in 1913. He was an officer in the Regular Forces (Suffolk Regiment), and was killed in action on the 18th of June, 1915, at Zillebeke, when serving with the British Expeditionary Force. He was twenty-two years of age.

CAPTAIN LESLIE WILLIAM WHITWORTH QUIN, M.C., was educated at Temple Grove and Felsted Schools. After serving in Child's Bank he went to South America, where he acquired a good business position. In October, 1915, he returned home, joined the Inns of Court O.T.C. and was commissioned in April, 1916, to the 27th Battalion Northumberland Fusiliers on active service. In October, 1916, he was awarded the Military Cross because "he led a raiding-party with great courage and skill, maintaining his position for one and a half hours, setting a splendid example to his men." He was promoted Captain in 1917, and was killed by a German sniper on the 24th of April of that year. His commanding officer said that "he died, as he had always lived, a magnificent pattern to all of us, and simply gave his life for his regiment." He was only twenty-three years of age.

LIEUTENANT CYRIL WILLIAM RENTON was formerly in practice as a solicitor, and was called to the Bar in 1913. When war was declared he joined the Inns of Court O.T.C. and became musketry instructor, being then forty-one years of age. Later he succeeded in being sent to France, where he went through six months active service, returning home after he had been wounded. He died on the 19th of July, 1917, aged forty-four, after two months illness, following wounds received in action. He served overseas in the 20th County of London Battalion.

LIEUTENANT WILLIAM KINGSLEY REYNOLDS was educated at Rugby, and Merton College, Oxford. He was engaged in business until the outbreak of war, when he enlisted as a private in the Public Schools Battalion. In October, 1914, he obtained his commission in the 6th Battalion Leicester Regiment. In July, 1915, he was promoted Lieutenant and was posted to the 1st Battalion Leicesters in France. On the 10th of September, 1915, during heavy shelling of the trenches at Wieltje, near Ypres, he gallantly went to the assistance of a wounded sergeant. He was instantly killed by a German shell. He was a first-class all-round athlete and a most promising officer. He had been admitted as a student in 1911, and was twenty-four years of age when he fell in action. He was an only son.

LIEUTENANT COSMO GEORGE ROMILLY was educated at Marlborough and New College, Oxford. He was a great grandson of Sir Samuel Romilly, who was Treasurer of Gray's Inn in 1803. He was called to the Bar in 1913, and joined the South Wales Circuit. He received his commission as Second-Lieutenant in September, 1914, in the 13th Battalion Sherwood Foresters, and was drafted to the 1st Royal Inniskilling Fusiliers in Gallipoli in May, 1915, as Lieutenant. He was in all the terrible fighting on that peninsula, being recommended for mention in despatches for great gallantry throughout the night of the 1st of July in bringing up reinforcements three times under heavy fire, and thus saving a critical situation. He was killed by an enemy sniper on the 11th of August, 1915, whilst out with a trench-digging party. His superior officer wrote that "he was an excellent officer, with great power of leading men. Fear was unknown to him; he was always calm and practical in emergency and a very lovable comrade." Before the War, during his short experience on circuit, Romilly had shown great promise as an advocate, and it was considered that he would maintain the great legal traditions of his distinguished ancestors. He was twenty-five years old when he laid down his life for his country.

PRIVATE CHARLES FREDERIC RORKE was an Advocate of the Supreme Court of the Transvaal and later of the Union of South Africa. He was farming in South Africa when he enlisted in the Divisional Signalling Company for service in the operations in German East Africa, where he died at Morogoro on the 1st of October, 1916. He was called to the Bar in 1899, and was fifty-one years of age at the time of his death on active service.

LIEUTENANT REGINALD HENRY SIMPSON was a Second-Lieutenant in the Westminster Dragoons when war broke out. He was promoted Lieutenant in October, 1914, and was posted to the 4th Battalion Lancashire Fusiliers, and was attached to the 2nd Battalion of that regiment, when he was killed in action at Pilckem, near Ypres, on the 9th of July, 1915, being then twenty-four years of age. He was admitted as a student in 1913.

LIEUTENANT DANIEL PIKE STEPHENSON of Kingston, Jamaica, was a Rhodes Scholar and undergraduate of Lincoln College, Oxford. He was admitted as a student at Gray's Inn in 1912. He enlisted as trooper in King Edward's Horse in August, 1914, receiving his commission in the 4th Staffordshire Regiment in that month. He was later attached to the 1st Cheshire Regiment in France. He was killed on the 24th of May, 1915, when leading a grenade party in re-taking a trench from the Germans. He was a fearless soldier and a born leader of men, and was recommended for the Military Cross. He was twenty-five years of age when he fell.

MAJOR ARTHUR JOHN NEWMAN TREMEARNE was educated at Melbourne University, became a scholar and prizeman of Christ's College, Cambridge, and received the degrees of M.A., LL.M., M.Sc. He saw active service in the first Victorian contingent in the South African War of 1899, and was there wounded. He served subsequently in West Africa, where he gained great knowledge of the Hausa language, which led to his obtaining the Hausa scholarship at Christ's College, Cambridge, where he became University Lecturer in that language. His published work in anthropology and folklore was considerable. Between 1909 and 1913 he was second in command of the 22nd London Regiment (The Queen's). He was attending the meetings of the British Association in Australia when war broke out, and immediately returned to England to join the 8th Battalion Seaforth Highlanders. He was shot through the heart when storming the German trenches at Loos on the 25th of September, 1915, being then thirty-eight years old. He was a clever, skilful soldier and leader of men. He was called to the Bar in 1912.

LIEUTENANT ELIAS TREMLETT, D.S.O., was educated at Crediton Grammar School and University College, London, obtaining the London University Law Scholarship in 1913. He was called to the Bar when serving in 1914, having previously won the Holt Scholarship and the Arden Scholarship at Gray's Inn. In September, 1914, he joined the Public Schools Battalion, and was commissioned in December, 1914, in the 9th Battalion Devon Regiment. In November, 1915, he was drafted to Egypt in the 4th Battalion Worcester Regiment, with which unit he was transferred in 1916 to France and promoted Lieutenant. In October, 1916, he was transferred to the Machine Gun Corps. On the 3rd of May, 1917, he was awarded the D.S.O. "He organized a bombing attack, and succeeded in working his way down 500 yards of the enemy's trench. Throughout the attack he showed admirable coolness and greatly stimulated the men under his command." On the 22nd of May, 1917, this gallant officer was killed by a heavy enemy shell, which came over and burst in the immediate vicinity of a group of officers and men talking in a quiet sector of the line. He lies in the British Cemetery at Mory Abbey, near Bapaume. He died at the age of twenty-seven.

CAPTAIN ALFRED COPLESTONE WALDEN-VINCENT was an undergraduate of Pembroke College, Cambridge, being called to the Bar in 1913. He was appointed Second-Lieutenant in the 5th Battalion Dorsetshire Regiment on the 1st of September, 1914, was promoted Captain on the 31st of December, 1914, and served with the Battalion in Gallipoli, where he was wounded on the 21st of August, 1915. He subsequently served in France, and was killed in action near Albert on the 26th of August, 1916, then being twenty-seven years of age.

SECOND-LIEUTENANT HENRY PERCY WEBER, a native of Demerara, British Guiana, was admitted a student in 1905. He joined the forces as Second-Lieutenant in the 7th King's Own Royal Lancaster Regiment in December, 1915. He was killed at Nieppe on the 16th of November, 1916, when leading his platoon over the parapet of the trenches in a raiding-party through the German lines. He was called to the Bar in 1909, and was thirty-one years of age when he fell in action.

LIEUTENANT ERIC CRAWCOUR WILSON was educated at Merchant Taylors' School and was in the service of the Anglo South American Bank in Paris when war commenced. He joined the Inns of Court O.T.C. as a cadet in December, 1914, and in April, 1915, was gazetted Second-Lieutenant in the 2nd Royal West Kent Regiment. In November, 1915, he went to India, being transferred in December, 1915, to Mesopotamia, where he served in many engagements and took part in the entry into Baghdad. He was killed near Mosul by a shell, after three years campaigning, on the 28th of October, 1918, aged twenty-seven. He was called to the Bar in 1913.

LIEUTENANT COLIN BASSETT WRONG, M.C., was educated at Queen's College, Demerara. He was admitted as a student at Gray's Inn in 1914. When war commenced he promptly enlisted in a Scottish regiment, and quickly received his commission in the 9th Bedfordshire Regiment. He was drafted to Salonica, where he won the Military Cross in 1917 for conspicuous gallantry and devotion to duty. He assisted in dragging a severely wounded man back a distance of 1500 yards under heavy fire, displaying great courage and coolness throughout. He was promoted Lieutenant in the 11th Battalion Munster Fusiliers, and served in Egypt and Palestine. He met his death in the course of the stubborn and successful fighting against the Turks near Jerusalem on the 28th of December, 1917. He was twenty-three years of age.

LIEUTENANT-COMMANDER JAMES DAWBARN YOUNG, R.N.V.R., was educated at St. Albans Grammar School, and adopted the profession of a Surveyor on leaving school. He was called to the Bar in 1906, and practised successfully on the South-Eastern Circuit. He was Examiner in Law to the Surveyors' Institution, and author of several legal works. In 1914 he joined the Royal Naval Reserve as Sub-Lieutenant, and was engaged in mine-sweeping. He was promoted Lieutenant and appointed to the command of a motor launch in the Dover Patrol, in which he did most effective work, including services of a very dangerous character. He was killed in the daring and gallant cutting-out expedition on Zeebrugge on the 23rd of April, 1918. It was his task, in a small craft, utterly unprotected against fire, to lay flares at the end of the Mole to act as navigation marks for the blockading ships. He laid one flare successfully, but the German guns blew it to pieces. He dashed in to lay another, but a salvo caught his little ship and sank her. He died riddled with shrapnel, and his country lost a very gallant officer. He was then forty-one years of age.

THE ROLL OF SERVICE OF MEMBERS OF THE SOCIETY WHO SERVED IN THE GREAT WAR

GIVING THEIR RANK ON JOINING; PERIOD OF SERVICE DURING THE WAR; UNIT; RANK WHEN DEMOBILIZED; DECORATIONS AND HONOURS

Compiled from returns made by members who had entered the Society before the Treaty of Peace, June 28, 1919.

Acting Rank is added in brackets in those cases where it was held during some part of the Service. Medals issued to large classes of all ranks are not included among "Decorations and Honours."

ABBOTT, CHARLES THEODORE: 2nd Lieut.; 1915–1919; Middlesex Regt.; LIEUT.

ADAM, JOHN FRASER: Private; 1915–1919; Royal Scots; Argyll and Sutherland Highlanders; LIEUT.

ADCOCK, WILLIAM ROBERT COLQUHOUN: Lieut.; 1914–1919; Nigeria Regt.; LIEUT.

ADDINSELL, THOMAS AUGUSTUS ARTHUR: Private; 1914–1919; Royal Fusiliers; Yorkshire Regt.; LIEUT.

AGAR, ARTHUR KIRWAN: Lieut; 1915–1919; R.A.S.C.; LIEUT. (ACTING-CAPT.).

ALLAN, ILLTYD DAVID: Private; 1914–1919; H.A.C.; Welch Regt.; CAPTAIN. M.C.

ANDRÉ, WILFRID JOSEPH GEORGE: Trooper; 1914–1919; Trinidad M.I.; Gloucester Regt.; LIEUT.

ANTELME, RAOUL: 2nd Lieut.; 1915–1916; Northumberland Fusiliers; 2ND LIEUT.

ARNETT, CHARLES WILLIAM: Lieut.; 1915–1919; R.A.O.C.; CAPTAIN (ACTING-MAJOR). M.C.

ASKINS, ROBERT ARTHUR: Lieut.; 1915–1919; R.A.M.C.; CAPTAIN.

ATKINSON, JOHN: Capt.; 1914–1919; R.A.S.C.; LIEUT.-COLONEL. D.S.O., O.B.E. Médaille de l'Alliance Française. Despatches (four times).

AUGUSTINE, VIVIAN OSBORNE: Trooper; 1917–1919; Indian Defence Force; TROOPER.

AUSTIN, EDWIN: Lieut.; 1914–1919; London Regt.; CAPTAIN.

BACK, ARTHUR WILLIAM: 2nd Lieut.; 1914–1919; Pembroke Yeomanry; Somaliland Camel Corps; CAPTAIN.

BAIRSTOW, FRED: Private; 1917–1919; Inns of Court O.T.C.; Cheshire Regt.; 2ND LIEUT.

BALL, GEORGE JOSEPH: Lieut.; 1914–1919; Intelligence Dept.; MAJOR. O.B.E. Despatches (twice).

BAMBER, PHILIP GORDON: 2nd Lieut.; 1914–1917; Devon Regt.; 2ND LIEUT.

BARNARD, HENRY WILLIAM: Private; 1914–1919; Inns of Court O.T.C.; R. W. Kent Regt.; LIEUT. (ACTING-CAPT.).

BARNETT, MAURICE: 2nd Lieut.; 1914–1918; 1st County of London Yeomanry; MAJOR.

BARROW, WYNFORD: 2nd Lieut.; 1914–1919; Deccan Horse; CAPTAIN.

BARRY, EDWARD PATRICK JOHN: Vety.-Major; 1914–1919; 2nd Life Guards; VETY.-LIEUT.-COLONEL.

BARTON, WILFRID ALEXANDER: 2nd Lieut.; 1915–1919; King's Liverpool Regt.; CAPTAIN. Despatches.

BATT, WILLIAM ELLIOTT: Major; 1914–1919; R.F.A.; LIEUT.-COLONEL. C.M.G. Despatches.

BECKE, JACK: Major; 1914–1919; Lancashire Fusiliers; MAJOR.

BECKER, JOHN NEILL: Private; 1918–1919; East Surrey Regt.; PRIVATE.

BENNETT, MARTIN GILBERT: Paymaster; 1914–1919; R.N.; PAYMASTER-COMMANDER. O.B.E.

BERLYN, BERNARD HENRY: Chaplain; 1914–1916; Royal Irish Rifles; 2ND LIEUT.

BERRY, ARTHUR: Private; 1914–1919; Welsh Horse; King's Liverpool Regt.; LIEUT. Despatches.

BIRKENHEAD, THE RIGHT HON. Viscount, Lord High Chancellor of Great Britain (see SMITH, The Right Hon. Sir Frederick Edwin).

BODKIN, HILARY WILLIAM ARCHIBALD: LIEUT.; 1917–1919; General List; LIEUT.

BONNER, CECIL ARTHUR JAMES: Private; 1915–1919; Inns of Court O.T.C.; Lancashire Fusiliers; CAPTAIN. Despatches.

BORTHWICK, GEORGE ARTHUR: Lieut.; 1915–1916; R.A.M.C.; CAPTAIN.

BOWEN, IVOR (a Master of the Bench, one of His Majesty's Counsel, now Judge of County Courts): Captain T. F. Reserve; 1914–1917; Major Commanding 15th Royal Welch Fusiliers (1st London Welsh); Lieut.-Colonel Commanding 18th Royal Welch Fusiliers (2nd London Welsh); LIEUT.–COLONEL.

BOWEN, JAMES BEVAN: 2nd Lieut.; Pembroke Yeomanry; R.A.F.; LIEUT.-COLONEL. O.B.E. Despatches.

BOX, FRANCIS WILLIAM: Gunner; 1914–1919; R.F.A.; GUNNER.

BRACE, IVOR LLEWELLYN: Private; 1916–1919; R.F.A.; 2nd LIEUT.

BRADDOCK, HENRY ALDWELL: 2nd Lieut.; 1915–1919; R.E.; R.A.F.; LIEUT. (ACTING-CAPT.).

BRANCH, CYRIL DENZIL: Lieut.; 1914–1919; R.A.S.C.; COLONEL. M.C. Chevalier de l'Ordre de la Couronne (Belgium). Croix de Guerre (Belgium). Despatches.

BREBNER, CHARLES STUART: Captain; 1914–1918; R.A.M.C.; CAPTAIN (ACTING-LIEUT.-COLONEL). D.S.O. Despatches (twice).

BRETHERTON, CYRIL H. E.: Private; 1916–1919; R.A.O.C.; LIEUT.

BRIDGEWATER, HOWARD: Gunner; 1916–1919; R.F.A.; R.A.F.; LIEUT.

BROADBENT, HAROLD: 2nd Lieut.; 1914–1919; Lancashire Fusiliers; CAPTAIN.

BROWN, ARTHUR TOM JOHN: Sergt.-Major; 1916–1919; R.A.S.C; CAPTAIN.

BROWN, HAROLD: Private; 1914–1919; King's Liverpool Regt.; The King's Own Royal Lancaster Regt.; LIEUT. (ACTING-CAPT.).

BROWN, JOHN: Captain; 1914–1919; 4th Northampton Regt.; LIEUT.-COLONEL. D.S.O. Order of St. Anne, with swords (Russia); Despatches (twice).

BUCKLEY, FRANCIS: Private; 1915–1919; Inns of Court O.T.C.; Northumberland Fusiliers; LIEUT. (ACTING-CAPT.). Despatches.

BULL, JAMES ROBINSON: A.B.; 1914–1919; R.N.V.R.; R.G.A.; LIEUT.

BULLOCK, WILLOUGHBY: Lieut.-Colonel; 1914–1919; R.A.M.C.; LIEUT.-COLONEL.

BURGIS, EDWIN COOPER: Lieut.; 1915–1919; R.A.S.C.; R.G.A.; CAPTAIN.

BURNET, EDWARD: Lieut.; 1914–1919; R.A.M.C.; LIEUT.

BUTLIN, PERCY: Private; 1914–1918; Cheshire Regt.; M.G.C.; LIEUT.

CAIN, ERNEST: 2nd Lieut.; 1916–1919; R.A.S.C.; LIEUT.

CAMPBELL, CECIL JAMES HENRY: Lieut.; 1914–1919; R.A.S.C.; MAJOR.

CAMPBELL, THOMAS: Lieut.; 1914–1919; Canadian R.A.M.C.; CAPTAIN.

CAMPBELL, WILLIAM GORDON: Captain; 1918–1919; R.M.L.I.; CAPTAIN.

CANTLIE, KEITH: Lieut.; 1914–1919; 103rd Mahrattas; CAPTAIN.

CARLETON, KEITH OSBORNE: 2nd Lieut.; 1915–1919; Indian Army; CAPTAIN.

CARPENTER, CHARLES HOWARD: Lieut.; 1918–1919; R.N.V.R.; LIEUT. O.B.E.

CARR, ARTHUR STRETTELL COMYNS: Private; 1918–1919; Inns of Court O.T.C.; PRIVATE.

CARRINGTON, REGINALD CHARLTON: Private; 1914–1919; Middlesex Regt.; South Wales Borderers; LIEUT. (ACTING-CAPT.).

CARTER, GERALD FRANCIS: Lieut.; 1914–1919; R.A.M.C.; LIEUT.-COLONEL. O.B.E.

CARTER, WILLIAM: Private; 1915–1918; Bedford Regt.; PRIVATE.

CHAMBERLAIN, JOHN ALFRED: Private; 1914–1919; London University O.T.C.; R.A.O.C.; CAPTAIN.

CHANCE, ERNEST WASHINGTON: Captain; 1914–1919; Kensington Rifles; LIEUT.-COLONEL. O.B.E.

CHETTLE, HENRY FRANCIS: Lieut.; 1914–1919; R.A.S.C.; MAJOR. O.B.E.

CHILCOTT, HARRY WARDEN STANLEY: Lieut.; 1914–1917; R.N.V.R.; R.N.A.S.; LIEUT.-COMMANDER.

CHRISTOPHER, CHARLES MORDAUNT DE AGUILAR: 2nd Lieut.; 1914–1919; Middlesex Yeomanry; R.F.A.; LIEUT.

CHURCHILL, LORD IVOR CHARLES SPENCER-: 2nd Lieut.; 1917–1919; R.A.S.C.; 2ND LIEUT.

CLARKE, SYDNEY ALFRED: 2nd Lieut.; 1915–1919; R.A.S.C.; MAJOR. Despatches.

CLIFFE, ERIC FRANCIS: Private; 1914–1919; Inns of Court O.T.C.; R.G.A.; CAPTAIN.

COLES, HERBERT SCAMMELL: Private; 1914–1919; H.A.C.; Middlesex Regt.; LIEUT.

COLLINGRIDGE, WILLIAM: Lieut.-Colonel; 1915–1919; R.A.M.C.; LIEUT.-COLONEL.

COLLINS, EDWARD HENRY: Corporal; 1914–1919; Civil Service Rifles; LIEUT.

CONNAUGHT, H.R.H. PRINCE ARTHUR FREDERICK PATRICK ALBERT OF, K.G., K.T., G.C.M.G., G.C.V.O., C.B., P.C. (Governor-General of South Africa; a Master of the Bench): Major, Royal Scots Greys; 1914–1919; served on Staff in France, 1914–1916, and on Canadian Staff Corps in France, 1917; MAJOR-GENERAL. Despatches.

COOKE, THOMAS ERIC: Trooper; 1914–1919; Essex Yeomanry; Royal Bucks Hussars; LIEUT. (ACTING-CAPT.).

COOKSON, CLAUDE EDWARD: Captain; 1917–1918; Gold Coast Regt.; MAJOR.

CORNISH, LIONEL JOHN: 2nd Lieut.; 1915–1919; R.A.S.C.; LIEUT.

CRESWELL, WILLIAM THOMAS: Captain; 1914–1919; R.E.; CAPTAIN.

CROSS, STANLEY THOMAS: Captain; 1914–1919; Gloucester Regt.; CAPTAIN. Despatches.

CROUCH, JAMES LEONARD: Lieut.; 1917–1919; General List; LIEUT.

CRUTTENDEN, REGINALD: Private; 1914–1919; Artists Rifles; M.G.C.; LIEUT. (ACTING-CAPT.).

CUMMINS, WILLIAM ASHLEY: 2nd Lieut.; 1914–1919; Oxford and Bucks Light Infantry; CAPTAIN.

CUTTER, ROY CARNEGIE: Private; 1914–1919; Royal Fusiliers; CAPTAIN.

D'APICE, JOHN EDMUND FRANCIS: Captain; 1914–1919; R.G.A.; LIEUT.-COLONEL. D.S.O. Order of the White Eagle, 4th class with swords (Serbia). Despatches (twice).

DAVIES, DAVID PERCY: Private; 1914–1919; Middlesex Regt.; Welch Regt.; CAPTAIN (ACTING-MAJOR). Despatches (twice).

DAVIES, HERBERT BARRS: Private; 1914–1919; Royal Fusiliers; Manchester Regt.; CAPTAIN.

DAVIES, JACK WALLIS: Private; 1915–1919; Inns of Court O.T.C.; The Buffs; LIEUT.

DAVIES, THOMAS RALPH DINGAD: 2nd Lieut.; 1914–1919; South Staffordshire Regt.; LIEUT. Despatches.

DAVIS, FRANCIS ROBERT EDWARD: Sub.-Lieut.; 1915–1919; R.N.A.S.; R.A.F.; MAJOR. O.B.E. Despatches.

DAVIS, REGINALD UNWIN: Assistant Clerk; 1914–1919; R.N.; PAYMASTER-LIEUT.-COMMANDER.

DAVY, THOMAS ARTHUR LEWIS: 2nd Lieut.; 1915–1919; R.F.A.; LIEUT. (ACTING-CAPT.).

DAWSON, GEORGE LOUIS: 2nd Lieut.; 1915–1919; R.F.A.; LIEUT.

DELL, THOMAS: Assistant Paymaster; 1914–1919; R.N.R.; PAYMASTER-LIEUT.

DENNY, EDWARD MAYNARD CONINGSBY: Private; 1914–1919; Inns of Court O.T.C.; Duke of Cornwall's Light Infantry; CAPTAIN. M.C. and Bar.

DERBYSHIRE, HAROLD: 2nd Lieut.; 1914–1919; R.G.A.; MAJOR. M.C.

DIAMOND, ABRAHAM SIGISMUND: Driver; 1916–1919; H.A.C.; DRIVER. M.M.

DICKSON, WILLIAM EVERARD: Private; 1914–1919; Lancashire Fusiliers; M.G.C.; MAJOR. M.C. and Bar. Despatches.

DINGLI, ADRIAN: 2nd Lieut.; 1914–1919; R.M.A. Research Dept.; CAPTAIN (ACTING-MAJOR). O.B.E.

DOCKRELL, KENNETH BROOKS: Private; 1918–1919; Royal Irish Fusiliers; PRIVATE.

DONALD, ALEXANDER GOSTLING: 2nd Lieut.; 1914–1919; R.F.A.; CAPTAIN.

DU CANN, CHARLES GARFIELD LOTT: Private; 1914–1919; Middlesex Regt.; CAPTAIN.

DUHAMEL, JEAN AUGUSTIN: Private; 1914–1919; French Staff; LIEUT. M.C.

DUKE, EDWARD: Captain; 1914–1919; Reserve of Officers; CAPTAIN. O.B.E. Despatches.

DUNCAN, ALEXANDER CHARLES: Lieut.; 1914–1919; R.A.V.C.; MAJOR. Despatches.

DUNCAN, NORMAN: Private; 1914–1919; Inns of Court O.T.C.; Dorset Yeomanry; LIEUT. M.C.

DUNSTAN, ROBERT: Lieut.; 1916–1917; R.A.M.C.; LIEUT.

EDWARDS, JOHN: Private; 1914–1919; 15th Royal Welch Fusiliers (1st London Welsh); MAJOR (ACTING-LIEUT.-COLONEL); D.S.O. Despatches.

EDWARDS-JONES, MALDWYN IVOR: Private; 1917–1919; Royal Welch Fusiliers; 2nd LIEUT.

ELIAS, WILLIAM ALFRED: 2nd Lieut.; 1914–1915; King's Liverpool Regt.; 2ND LIEUT.

ELLIOTT, MYLES LAYMAN FARR: Private; 1914–1919; Inns of Court O.T.C.; Gloucester Regt.; CAPTAIN.

ESSENHIGH, REGINALD CLARE: Private; 1914–1919; London University O.T.C.; Manchester Regt.; LIEUT. (ACTING-CAPT.).

EVANS, DAVID MORGAN: Private; 1915–1919; Artists Rifles; Welch Regt. LIEUT.

EVANS, GERALD ARTHUR: Captain; 1914–1919; Imperial Light Horse (S.A.); CAPTAIN.

FANNER, WILLIAM ROGERS: Private; 1914–1919; Inns of Court O.T.C.; Lancashire Fusiliers; MAJOR. M.C. Despatches.

FARADAY, WILFRED BARNARD: Private; 1914–1916; Bristol University O.T.C.; York and Lancaster Regt.; 2ND LIEUT.

FEE, WILLIAM GEORGE: Lieut.; 1915–1919; R.A.M.C.; CAPTAIN.

FIOR, LUCIEN: Private; 1917–1919; Middlesex Regt.; LANCE-CORPL.

FISHER, RONALD ARTHUR: Trooper; 1914–1919; Sussex Yeomanry; Royal Fusiliers; LIEUT.

FITZGERALD, SEYMOUR GONNE VESEY: 2nd Lieut.; 1918–1919; Indian Army; 2ND LIEUT.

FLEMING, SAMUEL: Lieut.; 1915–1919; General List; MAJOR.

FORBES, WILLIAM: Private; 1914–1919; Royal Fusiliers; Leicester Regt.; M.G.C.; CAPTAIN.

FORSTER, JOHN: Gunner; 1914–1919; R.G.A.; CAPTAIN.

FOSTER, WILFRED JUSTUS: Private; 1915–1917; R.A.M.C.; PRIVATE.

FRAZIER, ROWLAND WYNNE: O.S.; 1914–1919; R.N.V.R.; R.A.F.; CAPTAIN.

GALBRAITH, DAVID DUDLEY: Private; 1915–1919; Inns of Court O.T.C.; R.A.S.C.; CAPTAIN. Despatches.

GARVIN, HUBERT EVERARD: Private; 1914–1919; Queen Victoria's Rifles; West Yorkshire Regt.; LIEUT.

GAUSSEN, JAMES ARCHIBALD: Assistant-Paymaster; 1914–1919; R.N.; PAYMASTER-LIEUT.-COMMANDER.

GEE, ROBERT: R.Q.M. Sergt.; 1914–1919; Royal Fusiliers; R. W. Kent Regt.; CAPTAIN. V.C., M.C. Despatches (three times).

GIBB, ANDREW DEWAR: 2nd Lieut.; 1914–1919; Royal Scots Fusiliers; MAJOR. M.B.E.

GIBBINS, PERCY HEDON: 2nd Lieut.; 1914–1919; R.F.A.; LIEUT. (ACTING-MAJOR). M.C.

GODDING, JAMES: Lieut.-Colonel; 1914–1919; London Regt.; R.A.M.C.; COLONEL. O.B.E. Despatches (three times).

GOFFIN, SYDNEY: Assistant Financial Adviser, B.E.F., France; 1918–1919; HON. COLONEL. O.B.E. Despatches.

GOULDEN, ERNEST OSMUND: 2nd Lieut.; 1914–1919; R. W. Kent Regt.; LIEUT. M.C.

GRAHAM, CHARLES LESTER: Lieut.; 1914–1916; R.A.M.C.; CAPTAIN.

GRANT, CHARLES GRAHAM: Lieut.; 1914–1919; R.A.M.C.; LIEUT.-COLONEL.

GRAZEBROOK, HENRY BROOME DURLEY: 2nd Lieut.; 1916–1919; R.A.F.; LIEUT.

GRECH, WYNDHAM LEVY: 2nd Lieut.; 1916–1919; R.A.F.; CAPTAIN. Chevalier of the Order of the Crown of Italy.

GREENWOOD, ALFRED: Major; 1914–1916; R.A.M.C.; MAJOR.

GREENWOOD, THE RIGHT HON. SIR HAMAR, Bart. (a Master of the Bench, one of His Majesty's Counsel and Chief Secretary for Ireland): Captain; 1914–1916; Lieut.-Colonel Commanding 10th South Wales Borderers; Hon. Colonel Winnipeg Grenadiers; LIEUT.-COLONEL.

GRIFFITH-JONES, JOHN STANLEY: Private; 1914–1919; Inns of Court O.T.C.; South Wales Borderers; CAPTAIN.

GROVE, EDWARD THOMAS NEWCOMEN: 2nd Lieut.; 1914–1919; Royal Bucks Hussars; Egyptian Army; CAPTAIN.

GROVES, PERCY ROBERT CLIFFORD: Captain; 1914–1919; King's Shropshire Light Infantry; R.A.F.; COLONEL. C.B., C.M.G., D.S.O. Commander of the Legion of Honour. Despatches (three times).

GRUNDY, CLAUDE HERBERT: Private; 1914–1919; Canadian Forces; Bedford Regt.; LIEUT.

GUNN, HUGH: Captain; 1915–1916; Northumberland Fusiliers; CAPTAIN.

HAMER, HERBERT: Private; 1916–1919; Cheshire Regt.; R.E.; MAJOR. Despatches.

HAMILTON, ALLISTER McNICOLL: Private; 1914–1919; Inns of Court O.T.C.; Finsbury Rifles; LIEUT.

HAMPSON, STUART HIRST: 2nd Lieut.; 1915–1919; Lancashire Fusiliers; CAPTAIN. M.C.

HARDING, HARRY HARCOURT: Private; 1916–1919; King's Liverpool Regt.; Gordon Highlanders; CAPTAIN.

HARNETT, EDWARD ST. CLAIR: Private; 1914–1919; Queen's Westminsters; Black Watch; R.A.F.; MAJOR. O.B.E. Despatches.

HARRAGIN, WALTER: 2nd Lieut.; 1916–1919; R.F.A.; MAJOR. Despatches.

HARRIES, BERTRAM GEORGE GIBSON: Private; 1914–1919; Inns of Court O.T.C.; R.A.O.C.; CAPTAIN (ACTING-MAJOR). M.C. Despatches.

HARVEY, HENRY LESLIE: Private; 1917–1918; R.G.A.; PRIVATE.

HEALY, MAURICE FRANCIS: 2nd Lieut.; 1915–1919; Royal Dublin Fusiliers; LIEUT. (ACTING-CAPT.). M.C.

HEDLEY, JOHN FORSTER: Sub-Lieut.; 1915–1919; R.N.V.R.; R.A.F.; CAPTAIN. Despatches.

HENDERSON, PERCIVAL: 2nd Lieut.; 1915–1919; R.E.; CAPTAIN.

HENDRY, ARTHUR GEORGE LAUNCELOT: Captain; 1914–1919; The Buffs; Anglo-French Red Cross; CAPTAIN. Médaille de la Reconnaissance Française.

HENRY, FRANCIS JOSEPH: Lieut.; 1915–1919; R.A.M.C.; CAPTAIN. M.C.

HEPPEL, WALTER GEORGE: Engineer-Commander; 1914–1919; R.N.; ENGINEER-COMMANDER.

HERBERT-SMITH, GWENFFRWD MOSTYN: 2nd Lieut.; 1914–1919; 15th Royal Welch Fusiliers (1st London Welsh); M.G.C.; MAJOR.

HILBERY, GEORGE MALCOLM: A.B.; 1914–1919; R.N.V.R.; LIEUT.

HINDE, HARRY PERCY: 2nd Lieut.; 1914–1919; 10th London Regt.; CAPTAIN.

HOBSON, CHARLES MORTIMER: 2nd Lieut.; 1914–1919; South Lancs. Regt.; M.G.C.; LIEUT.

HODGE, CHARLES HELLYER: Private; 1915–1919; London Rifle Brigade; Tank Corps; CAPTAIN.

HODSON, JOHN: Sub-Lieut.; 1915–1919; R.N.V.R.; R.A.F.; CAPTAIN.

HOLT-HUGHES, THOMAS HUGHES: 2nd Lieut.; 1914–1919; Lancashire Fusiliers; CAPTAIN.

HOME, DOUGLAS RALPH: 2nd Lieut.; 1915–1919; R.E.; CAPTAIN.

HOPKINS, ERNEST LEWIS: Col.-Sergt.; 1916–1919; School of Musketry; R.A.F.; 2ND LIEUT.

HORNE, WILLIAM KENNETH: Private; 1916–1919; R.A.S.C.; LIEUT.

HUTCHENS, HAROLD JOHN: 2nd Lieut.; 1914–1916; R.A.M.C.; CAPTAIN.

INCLEDON-WEBBER, WILLIAM BEARE: Staff Sergt.; 1914–1919; School of Musketry; CAPTAIN.

ISHMAEL, GEORGE CLANSON: Private; 1914–1917; Uganda Volunteer Reserve; Intelligence Dept.; LIEUT.

IZOD, CHARLES LILBURN: Corporal; 1914–1919; East Surrey Regt.; SERGEANT.

JACOBSOHN, ARTHUR: 2nd Lieut.; 1917–1919; R.A.S.C.; LIEUT.

JALLAND, ARTHUR EDGAR: Private; 1915–1919; Manchester Regt.; R.G.A.; LIEUT.

JENKINS, WILLIAM LIONEL: 2nd Lieut.; 1917–1919; R.E.; CAPTAIN. Despatches.

JOHNSON, CHARLES BERNARD: 2nd Lieut.; 1914–1919; Lancashire Fusiliers; 2ND LIEUT.

JOHNSON, CLIFFORD OWEN: A.B.; 1914–1919; R.N.V.R.; A.B.

JOHNSON, ROBERT ARTHUR: Lieut.-Colonel; 1914–1919; 9th Hants; COLONEL. C.B.E.

KENDAL-GRIMSTON, HUGH DORRINGTON: 2nd Lieut.; 1914–1919; Royal Defence Corps; LIEUT.

KING, DAVID THOMSON: Sub-Lieut.; 1915–1919; R.N.V.R.; LIEUT.

KNIGHT, MELVILLE WHITMARSH: 2nd Lieut.; 1914–1919; Royal Warwicks; LIEUT.

LANCASTER, ROY CAVANDER: 2nd Lieut.; 1915–1919; The Buffs; LIEUT. (ACTING-CAPT.).

LANGLEY-SMITH, NELSON HUMPHRIES: Private; 1914–1918; Middlesex Regt.; Gloucester Regt.; LIEUT.

LANGLEY-TAYLOR, WILLIAM LAWRENCE: 2nd Lieut.; 1914–1919; R.F.A.; MAJOR.

LANGMAN, THOMAS WITHERIDGE: Private; 1914–1919; O.T.C.; Welch Regt.; CAPTAIN. O.B.E. Despatches.

LEACH, ROBERT WEBBER: 2nd Lieut.; 1914–1919; Lancashire Fusiliers; CAPTAIN.

LEES, SAMUEL: Engineer-Lieut.; 1915–1918; R.N.; ENGINEER-LIEUT.-COMMANDER.

LEGGE, PERCY AULAGNIER: Major; 1914–1919; Togoland Expeditionary Forces; MAJOR.

LIGHTFOOT, JOHN HENRY: Staff Surgeon; 1914–1919; R.N.; SURGEON-COMMANDER.

LIPSETT, LEWIS RICHARD: Lieut.; 1915–1919; R.A.S.C.; MAJOR.

LOSEBY, CHARLES EDGAR: 2nd Lieut.; 1914–1919; Lancashire Fusiliers; CAPTAIN. M.C.

LUCY, ARTHUR BERTRAM: 2nd Lieut.; 1914–1919; 4th City of London Regt.; CAPTAIN.

LUDLOW, RICHARD ROBERT: Private; 1915–1917; Inns of Court O.T.C.; Duke of Cornwall's Light Infantry; 2ND LIEUT.

LUTTER, WALTER FREDERICK: 2nd Lieut.; 1915–1919; Indian Army; CAPTAIN.

MACASKIE, CHARLES FREDERICK CUNNINGHAM: Private; 1916–1919; Essex Regt.; LIEUT. (ACTING-CAPT.).

MACASKIE, NICHOLAS LECHMERE CUNNINGHAM: Gunner; 1917–1919; R.G.A.; 2ND LIEUT.

McDOWELL, FRANK JOHN JAMES FOSTER: Lieut.; 1915–1919; Lancashire Fusiliers; CAPTAIN.

McNAIR, WILLIAM LENNOX: Private; 1914–1919; Artists Rifles; Royal Warwicks; LIEUT. (ACTING-CAPT.).

MANISTY, HENRY WILFRED ELDON: Fleet Paymaster; 1914–1919; R.N.; PAYMASTER-CAPTAIN. C.B., C.M.G.

MANLEY, NORMAN WASHINGTON: Gunner; 1915–1918; R.F.A.; GUNNER. M.M.

MAPLES, EDWARD WILLIAM: Captain; 1914–1918; Royal Welch Fusiliers; MAJOR. O.B.E.

MASON, JAMES MALCOLM: Lieut.-Colonel; 1915–1917; New Zealand R.A.M.C.; LIEUT.-COLONEL.

MEREWETHER, EDWARD ROWLAND ALWORTH: Surgeon; 1914–1919; R.N.; SURGEON-COMMANDER. Order of St. Sava, 4th class (Serbia). Despatches.

METCALFE, HERBERT: 2nd Lieut.; 1914–1917; Lancashire Fusiliers; LIEUT.

MIDDLETON, NOEL: Private; 1917–1919; Inns of Court O.T.C.; Highland Light Infantry; LIEUT.

MILLIGAN, HENRY JOSEPH: Lieut.; 1915–1919; R.A.M.C.; MAJOR. M.C. and Bar.

MORGAN, JOHN: Private; 1915–1918; Worcester Regt.; 2nd LIEUT.

MORRIS, ANTHONY J.; 2nd Lieut.; 1917–1919; R.A.F.; LIEUT.

MORRIS, NOAH: Lieut.; 1917–1918; R.A.M.C.; CAPTAIN.

MOSES, OWEN ST. JOHN: Major; 1915–1917; Indian Medical Service; MAJOR.

MOSS, JOHN: Private; 1916–1919; Somerset Light Infantry; 2ND LIEUT.

MULLER, JAMES ECKHARD: Trooper; 1914–1919; King Edward's Horse; R.F.A.; CAPTAIN. M.C.

MULLIGAN, ARTHUR DE WOLF: Lieut.; 1914–1919; R.N.V.R.; LIEUT.

MULLINS, CLAUD: Private; 1915–1919; Artists Rifles; R.A.O.C.; LIEUT.

NETHERSOLE, JOHN MAPLETOFT: Private; 1915–1919; Civil Service Rifles; LANCE-CORPORAL.

NEWBERRY, WILLIAM FREDERICK: Captain; 1914–1919; Queen's Royal West Surrey Regt.; CAPTAIN.

NICHOLAS, CYRIL WACE: Private; 1916–1919; King's Royal Rifles; LIEUT. Despatches.

NOLAN, HENRY GRATTAN: Private; 1916–1919; Inns of Court O.T.C.; Canadian Corps; CAPTAIN. M.C. Despatches.

NORRIS, HARRY HUGH: Private; 1917–1919; R.A.S.C.; PRIVATE.

OAKLEY, ROBERT O'FIELD: 2nd Lieut.; 1916–1919; R.A.O.C.; CAPTAIN.

O'CONNOR, DERMOT PATRICK JOSEPH: Lieut.; 1914–1919; East Surrey Regt.; CAPTAIN. M.C. Despatches.

O'CONNOR, EDWARD: Lieut.; 1914–1917; R.A.M.C.; CAPTAIN.

ODGERS, LINDSEY NOEL BLAKE: Private; 1914–1919; Inns of Court O.T.C.; Middlesex Regt.; CAPTAIN. M.C.

O'NEILL, GERALD MONTAGU: Private; 1915–1918; Artists Rifles; R.G.A.; CORPORAL.

O'SULLIVAN, DENNIS NEIL: Private; 1917–1918; Artists Rifles; PRIVATE.

OWEN, GORONWY: 2nd Lieut.; 1914–1919; 15th Royal Welch Fusiliers (1st London Welsh); MAJOR. D.S.O. Despatches (twice).

OXENHAM, EDWARD JOHN BARON: Private; 1914–1919; Inns of Court O.T.C.; R.A.O.C.; CAPTAIN (ACTING-MAJOR). M.C. Despatches (twice).

PAGET, CYRIL NEVIL: Captain; 1914–1919; 25th London Regt.; CAPTAIN.

PAINTON, WALTER: 2nd Lieut.; 1914–1919; R.A.S.C.; CAPTAIN (ACTING-MAJOR).

PARKER, HENRY ALBERT: Gunner; 1916–1919; R.G.A.; 2nd LIEUT.

PARRY, RONALD ERNEST LAMBERT: Private; 1918–1919; Oxford and Bucks Light Infantry; 2ND LIEUT.

PEREIRA, AELIAN WOODWARD McCARTHY: Private; 1914–1919; Queen Victoria's Rifles; Durham Light Infantry; LIEUT.

PETRIE, JAMES ALEXANDER: 2nd Lieut; 1917–1919; General List; LIEUT.

PHILLIPS, JOHN NICHOLSON ADDISON: Private; 1916–1919; Durham Light Infantry; LANCE-CORPORAL.

POCOCK, SYDNEY ELSDON: Lieut.; 1915–1919; R.A.S.C.; CAPTAIN (ACTING-MAJOR). O.B.E.

POYSER, KENNETH ELLISTON: Private; 1914–1919; Inns of Court O.T.C.; Loyal North Lancs; MAJOR (ACTING-LIEUT.-COLONEL). D.S.O. Despatches (three times).

PRESCOTT, WILLIAM HENRY: Captain; 1915–1916; R.E.; MAJOR.

PRETHEROE, EDWARD OWEN: 2nd Lieut.; 1915–1919; Northumberland Fusiliers; LIEUT. M.C.

PROSSER, CAMPBELL: Trooper; 1914–1919; Royal Gloucester Hussars; M.G.C.; LIEUT. Despatches.

PURCHAS, CHARLES: Lieut.-Colonel; 1914–1919; R.A.O.C.; COLONEL.

RAFFLE, ANDREW BANKS: Lieut.; 1914–1919; R.A.M.C.; CAPTAIN. M.C.

RATTRAY, ROBERT SUTHERLAND: Lieut.; 1914–1919; Togoland Field Force; LIEUT. M.B.E. Despatches.

REDHEAD, NORMAN RIDLEY FAIRBAIRN: Assistant-Paymaster; 1914–1919; R.N.; PAYMASTER-LIEUT.

REED, ARTHUR ERNEST: Mechanic; 1916–1919; R.A.F.; CAPTAIN.

REED, JOHN SEYMOUR BLAKE-: O.S.; 1916–1919; R.N.V.R.; LIEUT.

RENTOUL, GERVAIS SQUIRE: Lieut.; 1916–1919; General List; CAPTAIN.

RHODES, KENNETH: 2nd Lieut.; 1915–1919; R.F.A.; LIEUT.

RICH, THEODORE: Captain; 1914–1919; R.E.; MAJOR. O.B.E. Despatches.

RICHARDS, WILLIAM ISLWYN: Private; 1915–1919; Inns of Court O.T.C.; Tank Corps; LIEUT.

RITCHIE, ERNEST EDGAR: Private; 1915–1917; Inns of Court O.T.C.; Army Cyclist Corps; 2ND LIEUT.

RODGER, ROBERT STUART: Major; 1914–1917; R.A.M.C.; MAJOR.

ROGERS, MARTIN HOWARD: 2nd Lieut.; 1914–1919; Welch Regt.; LIEUT. (ACTING-CAPT.).

ROWSON, EDWARD: 2nd Lieut.; 1914–1919; South Lancashire Regt.; CAPTAIN.

SCOTT, DAVID JOBSON: Lieut.; 1914–1919; R.A.M.C.; CAPTAIN (ACTING-LIEUT.-COLONEL). M.C. O.B.E. Despatches.

SCRIVENER, WILLIAM KENT: Private; 1916–1919; Sherwood Foresters; R.E.; SAPPER.

SELLERS, FREDERIC AKED: Private; 1914–1918; The King's Liverpool Regt.; CAPTAIN. M.C. and two Bars.

SHARP, FREDERICK: Private; 1918–1919; R.A.F.; MECHANIC.

SHARPE, REGINALD TAAFFE: 2nd Lieut.; 1917–1919; Grenadier Guards, LIEUT.

SHARPUS, ARTHUR FREDERICK: 2nd Lieut.; 1917–1918; Indian Army; LIEUT.

SHAW, NORMAN MATTHEW: Gunner; 1915–1919; R.F.A.; LIEUT.

SHILLINGTON, CHARLES EDWARD: Private; 1914–1919; Royal Welch Fusiliers; LIEUT.

SMITH, ALLAN CHALMERS: Private; 1914–1919; King Edward's Horse; R.F.A.; LIEUT. (ACTING-CAPT.). M.C. Despatches (three times).

SMITH, DONALD CHRISTOPHER: 2nd Lieut.; 1915–1919; R.F.A.; LIEUT.

SMITH, FREDERICK: Private; 1915–1919; Inns of Court O.T.C.; Royal Warwicks; LIEUT.

SMITH, THE RIGHT HON. SIR FREDERICK EDWIN (now the Right Hon. Frederick, Viscount Birkenhead, Lord High Chancellor of Great Britain; a Master of the Bench); Senior Subaltern Oxfordshire Yeomanry, 1914; August, 1914, Director of Press Bureau; served in France as Major, G.S.O. 2, with Indian Corps until May, 1915; promoted Lieut.-Colonel on General Staff for special service in relation to Court Martial duties continuously discharged until January, 1919, when appointed Lord Chancellor; LIEUT.–COLONEL. Despatches.

SMITH, HAROLD (now Sir Harold Smith, M.P., and a Master of the Bench): Lieut.; 1914–1919; R.N.V.R.; LIEUT.

SMITH, ROBERT JAMES: Lieut.; 1918–1919; R.A.M.C.; LIEUT. O.B.E.

SMITH, VIVIAN FINDLAY: Private; 1915–1919; Artists Rifles; Hampshire Regt.; STAFF-SERGEANT.

SMITH, WILLIAM EDWARD: 2nd Lieut.; 1914–1919; R.A.S.C.; R.A.F.; CAPTAIN.

SOMERSET, RAGLAN HORATIO EDWYN HENRY: 2nd Lieut.; 1915–1919; R.A.S.C.; General List, Intelligence; CAPTAIN.

SPARKE, HENRY CHARLES: Captain; 1917–1919; Indian Army; CAPTAIN.

SPOONER, CHARLES AUGUSTUS: Captain; 1914–1919; R.A.M.C.; MAJOR.

STACPOLE, FREDERICK AUBREY: Private; 1914–1918; East Surrey Regt.; R.A.F.; CAPTAIN.

STALLARD, CHARLES FRAMPTON: Captain; 1914–1919; South African Forces; MAJOR (ACTING-LIEUT.-COLONEL). D.S.O. M.C. Despatches (twice).

STANLEY, THE HON. OLIVER FREDERIC GEORGE: 2nd Lieut.; 1914–1919; Lancashire Hussars; R.F.A.; CAPTAIN (ACTING-MAJOR). M.C. Despatches.

STEIN, HERBERT KATZEN: Private; 1916–1919; Artists Rifles; R.E.; LIEUT.

STEVENS, WILLIAM TINNEY: Private; 1914–1919; Royal Berkshire Regt.; Leicester Regt.; LIEUT. (ACTING-CAPT.). Despatches.

STODDART, JOHN: Staff Surgeon; 1914–1919; R.N.; SURGEON-COMMANDER. Order of St. Stanislas, 2nd class with swords (Russia).

STONEBRIDGE, JAMES BOYCE: 2nd Lieut.; 1915–1919; R.H.A.; LIEUT.

STRAY, CHARLES ASHTON: Private; 1918–1919; R.A.F.; PRIVATE.

STREDWICK, CECIL ARTHUR: Private; 1916–1919; Civil Service Rifles; Kensington Rifles; LIEUT.

TAYLOR, HUGH NEVILLE ADAM: Lieut.; 1914–1919; R.A.M.C.; MAJOR.

TAYLOR, WILLIAM: 2nd Lieut.; 1916–1919; T.F.R.; CAPTAIN.

TEMPLE, WILLIAM: 2nd Lieut.; 1915–1919; North Staffordshire Regt.; LIEUT.

TERRELL, COURTNEY: Private; 1914–1919; Inns of Court O.T.C.; CAPTAIN.

TERRELL, HUGH: 2nd Lieut.; 1915–1919; Indian Army; R.A.F.; LIEUT.

TETLEY, JOHN: Private; 1916–1919; Inns of Court O.T.C.; R.A.O.C.; LIEUT.

THOMAS, ALAN ERNEST WENTWORTH: Private; 1915–1919; Inns of Court O.T.C.; R.W. Kent Regt.; CAPTAIN. D.S.O., M.C. Despatches.

THOMAS, ARTHUR HERMANN: Lieut.; 1914–1917; Lancashire Fusiliers; MAJOR. Despatches (twice).

THOMAS, CHARLES WILLIAM: Private; 1914–1918; Inns of Court O.T.C.; Duke of Cornwall's Light Infantry; CAPTAIN.

THOMPSON, GEORGE HENRY MAIN: Sapper; 1916–1919; R.E.; LIEUT.

TIMMIS, JOHN VERNON: Captain; 1914–1917; Reserve of Officers; East Lancs Regt.; CAPTAIN.

TUCKER, WILLIAM THORNTON: Trooper; 1914–1919; Australian Light Horse; R.F.A.; CAPTAIN.

TURNER, REGINALD BRYETT, A.B.; 1915–1919; R.N.V.R.; R.G.A.; LIEUT.

VAN SERTIMA, SYDNEY JACOB: Private; 1915–1919; Middlesex Regt.; Manchester Regt.; CORPORAL.

VAN SOMEREN, WILLIAM VERNON LOGAN: 2nd Lieut.; 1914–1919; 9th Royal Fusiliers; LIEUT.-COLONEL. D.S.O., M.C. Belgian Croix de Guerre. Despatches (twice).

VAUGHAN, REGINALD CHARLES: Trooper; 1914–1919; Dragoon Guards; R.A.F.; CAPTAIN. M.C.

WALLACE, GERALD DOUGLAS HAMILTON: Lieut.; 1914–1917; R.A.M.C.; CAPTAIN.

WALSH, ERNEST PERCIVAL: 2nd Lieut.; 1916–1919; General List; CAPTAIN.

WARLOW, ARTHUR LEONARD: Coy.-Sergt.-Major; 1915–1918; School of Musketry; COY.-SERGT.-MAJOR.

WARRACK, JAMES STRATTON: Major; 1914–1918; R.A.M.C.; LIEUT.-COLONEL.

WATSON, JOHN BERTRAND: Private; 1916–1919; Artists Rifles; CAPTAIN.

WATSON, WILLIAM TREVOR: Private; 1917–1919; R.A.F.; CAPTAIN.

WATT, EDWARD WILLIAM: Captain; 1914–1919; 4th Gordon Highlanders; MAJOR (ACTING-LIEUT.-COLONEL).

WELLS, HENRY BENSLEY: 2nd Lieut.; 1914–1919; R.F.A.; LIEUT.

WELLSTEED, PERCY THOMAS: Private; 1914–1919; Civil Service Rifles; Monmouth Regt.; LIEUT.

WHARTON, LOUIS EDGAR: Driver; 1915–1919; H.A.C.; R.H.A.; 2ND LIEUT.

WHITTALL, LEONARD RICHARD: Private; 1918–1919; Worcester Regt.; LANCE-CORPORAL.

WILD, JAMES ANSTEY PRESTON: 2nd Lieut.; 1914–1919; Yorkshire Regt.; CAPTAIN.

WILLCOCK, PERCY DOUGLAS: Private; 1915–1919; Inns of Court O.T.C.; R.A.F.; LIEUT.

WILLIAMS, ALURED HUMPHREY: Lieut.; 1914–1919; R.A.S.C.; CAPTAIN.

WILLIAMS, SAM: Private; 1914–1919; Welch Regt.; LIEUT.

WILSON, DANIEL MARTIN: 2nd Lieut.; 1914–1916; 9th Royal Inniskilling Fusiliers; CAPTAIN.

WITHERINGTON, ARTHUR SIMPSON: 2nd Lieut.; 1916–1919; R.F.A.; LIEUT.

WONTNER, ADRIAN RUSSELL: 2nd Lieut.; 1916–1918; General List; CAPTAIN.

WOOD, MURDOCH McKENZIE: 2nd Lieut.; 1914–1919; Gordon Highlanders; R.A.F.; MAJOR. O.B.E.

WORSWICK, THOMAS: 2nd Lieut.; 1916–1919; R.A.F.; MAJOR. O.B.E.

WREFORD-GLANVILL, HEYMAN WREFORD: Private; 1915–1919; Inns of Court O.T.C.; R.A.S.C.; CAPTAIN. French Silver Medal of Honour. Despatches.

WYNN-WERNINCK, FREDERIC CORBET: Private; 1916–1919; Artists Rifles; General List; LIEUT.

YOUNG, KEITH RYMER: 2nd Lieut.; 1914–1919; Lancashire Fusiliers; Royal Welch Fusiliers; LIEUT.

YOUNG, SIDNEY MICHAEL: Private; 1918–1919; Inns of Court O.T.C.; LANCE-CORPORAL.

YULE, ROBERT ABERCROMBY: Captain; 1914–1918; 8th Rajputs; Indian Political Dept.; MAJOR.

MASTERS OF THE BENCH OF GRAY'S INN DURING THE WAR

IN THE ORDER OF THEIR ELECTION TO THE BENCH

H.R.H. THE DUKE OF CONNAUGHT, *K.G., K.T., G.B.E.*

H.R.H. PRINCE ARTHUR OF CONNAUGHT, *K.G., K.T., C.B.*

THE RT. HON. SIR EDMUND BARTON, *G.C.M.G.* (*Honorary. Died* 1920.)

THE RT. HON. SIR WILFRID LAURIER, *G.C.M.G.* (*Honorary. Died* 1919.)

THE HON. ALFRED DEAKIN. (*Honorary. Died* 1919.)

THE RT. HON. WILLIAM MORRIS HUGHES. (*Honorary. Prime Minister of the Commonwealth of Australia.*)

JOHN ROSE.

HIS HONOUR JUDGE JAMES MULLIGAN, *K.C.*

MILES WALKER MATTINSON, *K.C.* (*Recorder of Blackburn.*)

SIR LEWIS COWARD, *K.C.* (*A Railway and Canal Commissioner.*)

CHARLES ALFRED RUSSELL, *K.C.*

THE HON. SIR MONTAGUE LUSH. (*A Justice of the High Court.*)

HERBERT PARKER REED, *K.C.* (*Died* 1920.)

THOMAS TERRELL, *K.C.*

WILLIAM TYNDALL BARNARD, *K.C.*

THE RT. HON. SIR DUNBAR PLUNKET BARTON, BART., *K.C.* (*Lately a Justice of the High Court in Ireland.*)

THE RT. HON. SIR HENRY DUKE. (*A Lord Justice of Appeal: now President of the Probate, Divorce and Admiralty Division.*)

THE RT. HON. SIR JAMES HENRY MUSSEN CAMPBELL, BART. (*Lord Chancellor of Ireland,* 1918.)

HERBERT FRANCIS MANISTY, *K.C.* (*Recorder of Berwick-upon-Tweed.*)

EDWARD CLAYTON, *K.C.*

WILLIAM JOHN REYNOLDS POCHIN.

ARTHUR EDMUND GILL. (*Metropolitan Magistrate.*)

EDMUND FRANCIS VESEY KNOX, *K.C.* (*Died* 1921.)

THE RT. HON. SIR RICHARD ATKIN. (*A Lord Justice of Appeal.*)

THE RT. HON. SIR WILLIAM PATRICK BYRNE, *K.C.V.O., C.B.*

THE RT. HON. VISCOUNT BIRKENHEAD. (*Lord Chancellor,* 1919.)

HIS HONOUR JUDGE JOHN WILLIAM McCARTHY.

MONTAGU SHARPE, *K.C.*

GEORGE RHODES, *K.C.* (*Recorder of Oldham.*)

THE HON. SIR ARTHUR GREER. (*A Justice of the High Court.*)

TIMOTHY MICHAEL HEALY, *K.C.*

CHARLES HERBERT-SMITH.

HENRY WINCH. (*Died* 1917.)

HIS HONOUR JUDGE IVOR BOWEN, *K.C.*

SIR ALEXANDER WOOD-RENTON.

WILLIAM CLARKE HALL. (*Metropolitan Magistrate.*)

CECIL HENRY WALSH. (*A Judge of the High Court, North-Western Provinces, India.*)

ROBERT ERNEST DUMMETT. (*Recorder of South Molton.*)

THE RT. HON. SIR HAMAR GREENWOOD, BART., *K.C., M.P.*

THE RT. HON. MR. JUSTICE SAMUELS. (*A Justice of the High Court in Ireland.*)

INDEX

www.ingramcontent.com/pod-product-compliance
Ingram Content Group UK Ltd.
Pitfield, Milton Keynes, MK11 3LW, UK
UKHW012215240726
13966UKWH00003B/765